BEYOND ANXIETY

WHAT TO EXPECT ON YOUR PATH TO FREEDOM

Contents

Introduction

A life filled with anxiety is no life at all. However, life after anxiety is purposeful and unique. Unique in the sense that daily life is no longer lived within the cycle of "robotic" consciousness—the kind that we see all around us. We're no longer the blind leading the blind. Instead, we are like eagles gliding effortlessly high above with the ability to see and feel all of life unfolding at once.

Beyond anxiety, we are free to become whoever we wish to be because the fear of shame, guilt, and humiliation is no longer present. We stop caring about things we once viewed as being important. We have come full circle to the realization that our irrational fears gave us something to occupy our time, but nothing more.

Beyond anxiety, we understand that fear is hard-wired within us all, but irrational fear is learned. We understand how the dire need for control is just a protective mechanism activated by the subconscious, which keeps us craving more suffering. But why would anyone crave suffering, you may ask? Because it's a more certain place to live in than love, creativity, and even sound health. Some people believe these things will be taken away as swiftly as they show up, and most people fight to keep what they have out of fear of losing it all. Staying on the topic of control for a moment, did you know that your mental, emotional, behavioral, and imaginative habits are also a way of tapping into a sense of control over your life? There's a small conscious part of you that wants to rid yourself of things like catastrophic thought patterns, distraction techniques, energy vampires, your job, the daily lack of action you take over your inner healing journey, etc. However, all of those things give the subconscious mind/body a sense of certainty and control, and giving them up would mean death. That's why you seem to always come full circle back to your old habits—they give you a sense of identity, which, in turn, is approved by a society that believes suffering is inevitable. Heck, to society, inner peace is a strange and misunderstood thing.

Beyond anxiety, our self-worth is cemented, and our egos begin dissipating. No longer do we fight to be first in line at the grocery store or place our happiness on whether or not our favorite sports team wins. No, we are no longer that childish; instead, we are becoming more childlike, and it's a beautiful thing to witness and be a part of. Most people walking the planet today are no more mentally and emotionally mature than a 12-year-old (me included until around the age of 32). They live by the same belief systems they held when they were children and have never taken the time to upgrade those beliefs.

Before anxiety, there is purity. During anxiety, there is inner and outer chaos and confusion. After anxiety, there is ease and trust. This is a book about the afterlife—life after the life we thought was real for us. The best way to describe this transition from the artificial inner world to the natural world is to label it an awakening—an awakening to much more than what we thought was possible for us. After unconsciously living under the direction of our authority figures for so long, this awakening leads us to many unknown places. We find ourselves slowly drifting away from the comfort zones we have wasted too much time and energy on. A comfort zone is surely not just an environment; it's a way of thinking. It's our core belief system. It's our verbal expressions, our identity, and our imagination.

Beyond anxiety, we tear these old ways up and embrace spontaneity once again—something we didn't think we even had for a long time.

Beyond anxiety, we realize that anxiety is not a sign of weakness, and healing is not a sign of a journey completed. Instead, anxiety is a stepping stone to the truth about us and life, and healing is a sign of trusting in the unfolding of life once again. Trust is something we can all achieve, but only if we are willing to sacrifice our old ways of perceiving and living. Trusting in whatever life throws at us means we no longer separate things between good and bad. We are free from putting separate experiences in their individual places, and we see it all as life. When the leaves on a tree begin falling, the tree does not fear loss or death. Rather, the tree stands tall and fully accepts the changes made to it from day to day, season to season. We are becoming more like those very trees by the day—rooted, connected, and accepting of all that life offers us.

Beyond anxiety, the mind is no longer the body; it leads the body. We no longer allow our feelings to turn into emotions. From time to time, we may still get a feeling through our primal drives directed by our reptilian brain; however, we have the capability to tap into other perceptual options. We perceive as we are, not how the world wants us to perceive the situation anymore. As we move along this healing path, we strengthen our thinking and no longer rely on replaying the same old thought patterns. Our intuition is also strengthened, leading us to want to explore life more and more. Ah, yes, the curiosity of a young, uncorrupted child. What a beautiful sight. Age no longer gets in the way of what's right for us. We begin to understand that, through the power of intention, we can allow the answers we seek to come to us in time, and we no longer feel the need to find them at this very moment.

Beyond anxiety, we are in what I like to call a "flow state." There is no longer a need to separate our meditation time from our daily life since we are already in meditation all day long. We are deeply connected to the ground as we walk, the wind as it blows, and the people we talk to, and fear takes a back seat (way back). During anxiety, we suppressed our ideas, words, feelings, and emotions—everything. Beyond anxiety, we smile when we want to, say what comes to our heart, and express love for nature the way we always wanted to. Suppression is replaced by expression, and it gathers momentum, which begins affecting those around us. When two nervous systems are within each other's electromagnetic energy fields, they communicate with one another below the level of conscious awareness. When this unconscious communication takes place, it leads to a third effect, a mood. So, rest assured, you are saving humanity simply by defying the old you and embracing the new and all that comes with it.

During an anxiety disorder, we know too much and understand too little.

Beyond anxiety, we recognize that we already have all the answers within us, and this takes priority over the information we hear from the outside. This leads us right back into the flow state, as we believe more and more that we can come up with our own conclusions. No longer do we rely on information overload to heal us automatically; we are much smarter than that now. Hope is now seen as a starting point to healing but not a practical long-term strategy. Beyond anxiety, we stop waiting for it to happen, and we make it happen. So, let's continue to make it happen together through this valuable book you have in front of you.

I'm going to help you understand what is happening to you while you're on this healing journey. Some of these inner and outer occurrences may lead back to anxiety if we allow them to. But if we can truly embrace change and all the confusion that comes with it, we can tap back into an unconditional feeling of love toward it all. We can truly become more than anxiety with every passing day. Before you embark on this journey with me beyond anxiety, reflect back now on how far you've actually come. Is it quite a bit farther than you originally thought? I thought so.

Let us go beyond.

Chapter 1 – The Anxiety Blessings

It is truly a blessing to have gone through anxiety and come out the other side. There can be no light without the darkness, and there can be no silence without the chaos. Anxiety shows us what a dark and chaotic life is really like. For that, we must be grateful because where else would we be able to learn the lessons we have? Certainly not in a classroom or through our parents—they are still stuck in their old ways believing that you can never teach an old dog new tricks. Bless them, forgive them; their intentions are good. There are plenty of aspects to this recovery journey that we must bring to our awareness so that gratitude can override regret. Never get caught up in the amount of time you wasted with anxiety; the time was not wasted at all.

The Value of Life

Life beyond anxiety has tremendous value. Each day comes with fresh opportunities and surprises that start to feel like they manifest effortlessly. With every moment that passes, we truly fall in love with our accomplishments and our mistakes. Compare this to a time when perfectionism would not allow mistakes to enter your day. Beyond anxiety, perfectionism is now seen as investing your energy unwisely. Since we only have a finite amount of energy and willpower each day, we are now becoming pickier as to where it is focused.

As the value of life in all aspects grows, little things are no longer big things. When we come across situations that would normally suck us into fear, anger, blame, shame, or any other feeling, another voice within shows up as well. This voice is not the one coming from our heads, but rather from our hearts, and it guides us back to the truth of what life is. As our intuition begins overtaking our intellect, we find ourselves sacrificing what others would deem as our intelligence for something much greater—unconditional love.

Beyond anxiety, we literally begin feeling "less smart." With this transition comes a sense of loss. That sense of loss is what commonly brings people back to the addiction to suffering and a life of anxiety. Since we instinctually resist anything that goes against what we believe to be true, what others may think of us, or what we deem to be a part of our identity, we must decide between growing our intuition and acting on it or reverting back to our intellect and allowing overthinking to take over once again.

Overthinking is a comfort zone and a defense mechanism to change.

It's something many people turn to in order to not have to face the very thing they need to address. Overthinking buys a person time, and with time comes the temporary subsiding of the symptoms they repeatedly feel. These symptoms come around full circle, of course, many times stronger and louder as time goes on. You and I, though, are willing to continue to see the value of letting go. Letting go of the old can only be done by embracing the new and all that comes with it. The new, in this context, is everything you have yet to discover about yourself and life. The value of life increases with every new empowering idea you build on. These ideas, over time, turn into belief systems that affect you emotionally and spiritually. Nothing happens by chance; there is an energetic buildup and a progression to everything that happens in our physical reality. Your recovery is not an accident; it is based on the dissatisfaction you felt around how you were living that fueled you to understand what you couldn't at the time. This led you to take the consistent action necessary to change your identity.

The Value of Creativity

Have you noticed that you're becoming more and more interested in things you put on the shelf because of anxiety? That's no accident. The creative parts of yourself that have been neglected are longing for your attention now that the way you see yourself is changing. Because of anxiety, seriousness overtook fun, and that limited your inner resources. The more serious someone is, the less chance new beliefs can be formed. This is due to the power of neuroplasticity—the ability to alter our brain's neural wiring and learn new things. Now that you are placing less importance on things like that bigger house, the new car, the fancy clothes, etc., you are tapping back into your creativity, which is a beautiful thing. Creativity arises in a host of different ways that are unique to the individual. Some people may find themselves singing or dancing more. Others may begin writing that book they always wanted to. Some may start writing poems, and others might engage in painting. These inspiring crafts are often seen as useless endeavors by society, activities that must be replaced with a relentless focus on furthering our careers. Beyond anxiety, though, we recognize the importance of such creativity. Our priorities are beginning to shift away from pleasing others and building their dreams to self-care and tapping into our hidden talents.

Self-Care is Certainly Not Selfishness

In the past, we thought this was the case, but no more. We are beginning to understand the domino effect that arises when we take care of our own needs first. As we do, we inspire others to do the same. We become thinkers and not reactors anymore, artists rather than human robots, and life begins to have meaning once again.

The Value of Laughter

Have you also noticed certain human responses, like laughter, that you gradually fell out of touch with? I remember having a massive epiphany one day when I realized that I had to relearn how to laugh (along with many other things, of course). There was a time during anxiety when I believed laughter needed to be earned, seriousness led to progress (whatever that meant), and a sense of ease might lead to something catastrophic. Anxiety makes you feel like you need to stand guard at every turn just in case. But in case of what? What was is there to fear in the end anyway? Dying? We are all headed that way anyway, so why worry about it? I am at the point where I'm becoming more and more curious each day as to what's on the other side of this life. Imagine that ... curiosity over death, what a revelation.

Back to laughter, all fears have an accompanying feeling somewhere in the body, and if those feelings continue to compound, a person will become completely out of touch with who they really are. These feelings use up units of energy and weigh a person down more and more as their anxiety lives on. This is where the feeling of being wired but tired arises (daily visits between anxiety and depression). During anxiety, we are our artificial selves; beyond anxiety, we are back to our natural selves, and that comes with the ability to laugh again. Laughter arises because of the shift in emotional states that we feel. Moving from a non-trusting place to a trusting place loosens up the rigidity we have become accustomed to in our bodies and lengthens our breathing patterns. From this place, we can begin ridiculing our old fears and appreciating every opportunity to laugh again.

The Value of Anger

Anxiety teaches us the value of anger. I can hear you now. Yes, it's absolutely true. Anger can become a great motivator if we use it properly. First, what is anxiety? In my eyes, anxiety is a symptom of unresolved past traumas. They are stored and compounding in the three processors we have within our bodies: the brain, heart, and gut. These are like zip files on a desktop computer—files that hold tons of information connected to one topic. These zip files are also stored in the body of an anxiety sufferer. They become louder (symptoms) over time when the subconscious wants the conscious mind to do something different rather than continuing to stuff them down. Small fragments of these energies in the body become discharged from time to time—at the gym during a workout, at a concert, in a pub, or at a sporting event, for example. These experiences temporarily make the anxiety sufferer feel better. But the trauma-based zip files will again show up via mental, emotional, and physical symptoms if they are not resolved and discharged. (My second book, *F*ck Coping Start Healing*, talks in depth about emotional reframing to resolve these past traumas for good.)

So, where does anger fit into this scenario? We human beings are hard-wired to move toward pleasure and away from pain. This means that when we associate enough pain to living in a way we don't want to, we can begin taking the necessary action to change it. I bet this has happened in your own life. You got to the point I like to call "the point of no return," where you were willing to grip the edge of a sword to keep yourself from drowning and pull yourself back up. You felt that much dissatisfaction.

Remember, there is no such thing as a bad behavior or a bad feeling. The question is, does it help you get the result you want? So, anger certainly has its time and place to be used to motivate and to move away from pain and toward pleasure. Continue making it your friend when the timing is right.

The Value of Tonality

Going beyond anxiety means understanding the importance of tonality. The tones that are connected to the ideas you hear (your own or others) will affect you differently. An amazing lesson that anxiety taught me, and possibly you as well, is that tones go directly to the reptilian brain (responsible for our primal drives, our survival). That means when you hear something, the words aren't affecting you as much as the person's tone of voice. Add to the power of tonality the recognition that a fearful idea is being preached by an authority figure such as your parents or a doctor, and you have a recipe for an intense emotional experience that will most likely be stored in the memory files within your body.

Living beyond anxiety teaches us not to take ideas seriously anymore.

This even applies to our own thoughts. We get around 60,000 thoughts and ideas daily, and many of them are the same ones being played out on an endless loop. When we go beyond anxiety and begin living with a sense of inner peace, those ideas—and the tonality that comes with them—change. These changes lead to us becoming more interested in some ideas over others, and wherever our focus and attention goes is where our emotions will flow toward. The next time you get an idea you're sure you don't want to turn into a belief, imagine that Daffy Duck is saying it. No one takes Daffy Duck seriously unless, of course, you have had a traumatic experience with him in the past. When I do personal one-on-one sessions with people who are ready to go beyond anxiety, I usually frame their deepest concerns in a way that brings neutrality rather than fear within the first 5 minutes. This "reframe" catches them off guard because they have programmed themselves to believe that their internal or external problem is a monster of a challenge. But the moment I can tweak their perception so we can experience the feeling without the added emotion backing it up, we open the gates to healing. I do not approach this reframe logically or rationally; that wouldn't come with the strength it needs to begin the reconditioning process. Instead, I use cartoon characters, imagery exercises, funny animals, stories, tonality, and more … anything to get a *state break* within them. Why do I do this? Because if you give an anxiety sufferer what they expect, they will never heal. The key is to give them something unexpected so that they question what it is you just revealed to them. Confusion can be a powerful tool for any coach out there looking to help others right from the start.

Beyond anxiety, we are clearly recognizing a transition in the tonality of our inner dialogue also. Sufferers will repeatedly ask themselves questions regarding a catastrophic scenario that may play out in the future, which leads to their tonality being more high pitched (questions). Those who are on the path of healing find that their tonality is much more neutrally pitched, signifying a statement rather than a question. An example of this could be:

During anxiety — "If my bodily symptoms arise today, will I be able to function?"

Beyond anxiety — "Even if my bodily symptoms arise, I'll be able to function just fine."

Notice the difference in tonality toward the end of each. Healing anxiety allows us to become progressively more aware of what may pull us back into inner distress and what will keep us free.

The Value of Intention

Intention is a specific target that is aligned with our personal goals. Beyond anxiety, we recognize the importance of aligning with the right intention at the beginning of each day rather than allowing our subconscious to dictate what that intention might be. Here is an example of a conscious intention rather than an unconscious intention in my own transition away from anxiety:

Conscious intention (beyond anxiety) — "I will bring the mindset of calm awareness with me today."

Unconscious intention (during anxiety) — "I will bring the mindset of frantic awareness with me today."

Notice the differences in how the day will pan out depending on your intention to start the day. Of course, when you are beyond anxiety, you can bring a separate intention to separate situations you'll face throughout the day. The one that helped me, in general, was certainly the intention of calm awareness.

Calm awareness is an emotionally neutral recognition of what is taking place internally and externally. In contrast, frantic awareness is run by the emotional brain dedicated to keeping the person in a never-ending cycle of fight, flight, or, potentially, freeze.

In a world of robotic consciousness where most people react based on an urge or feeling, they are in frantic awareness. They have no control over what they can control on the inside because there is not yet the recognition that some other way of being is possible. Intention comes before skill sets in my world because a skill set may temporarily induce a mental and emotional shift in an anxiety sufferer. But without the proper intention that is emphasized with feeling daily, the changes made from the skill set itself will not gain any momentum. An anxiety sufferer will find creative (often unconscious) ways of going back to suffering until they take power back from their anxious emotional states. And it begins with intention.

The Value of Congruence

Congruence is the ability to have all the different parts of us working together toward one ultimate goal. Beyond anxiety, we have a sense of this connection getting stronger by the day. Here are the parts of us that find congruence along the healing journey:

- Our **thoughts** are coming from us alone, and our **perceptions** are becoming more neutral.
- Our **words** are based on what we feel is best to express in that moment rather than what may or may not be accepted by others.
- Our **imagination** is much more consciously run (what we want) rather than unconsciously run (what we do not want).
- Our **emotional states** are hovering between neutral and pleasant rather than staying stuck in negative states and, therefore, a low vibration.
- Our **belief systems** are our own rather than those of our parents, friends, or other authority figures.
- Out **behaviors** are aligned with the identity we want to create for ourselves.

When we are beyond anxiety, we feel like a fast-moving train that only uses the brakes temporarily. Everything is moving together toward one outcome, and that outcome is to live a life of inner peace and purpose. Beyond anxiety, we sense when one of these parts is not on board with the others, and we do something about it.

If it is our verbal communication with others, we consciously begin expressing the words that align with our goals, for example. We are then back in energetic alignment with who we want to be and what we want to manifest in our lives. It's like an airplane that cruises within that ideal flying height where it is very fuel-efficient and glides effortlessly.

As we move through our day, we must acknowledge that every challenge we face is a test. That test may come in the form of a thought, an uncomfortable image from your past, a loss of some kind, or being criticized by others … anything. These tests are not the same kinds of tests you took back in high school, though. There is no passing or failing grade. There is only awareness, a behavior connected to your intention, and a feeling of letting go of the need for certainty within this situation.

Failure cannot exist within a person who deems every experience as simply life itself.

When we are beyond anxiety, we no longer stay in the realm of fear for too long. Instead, we consciously or even unconsciously feel like something is off, and we do something about it. But there's another level to healing—a place where the person has already integrated mental, behavioral, verbal, and imagery-based changes into their lives and has created such a flow state that it's unnecessary to do anything in a moment of fear. When you get to this stage in the healing journey, doing nothing about a challenging situation is actually doing something. You trust that inaction is as valuable, if not more so than a responsive action. You are so well practiced and so comfortable in your own mind, body, and spirit at this point that nothing can take you out of who you've worked to become.

Summary:

As you can see, going beyond anxiety and staying on this inspired healing path comes with many beautiful lessons. The knowledge you need is gained from others, but the wisdom necessary to promote inner love and healing comes from you. Be grateful for these and the many other lessons that anxiety has taught you and will teach you. Never allow yourself to look back and fall back into helplessness and a victim-like state; only look back to see how far you've come. Take a few moments right now, before moving on, to think about some of the lessons anxiety has taught you. How has it bettered you, and how has it challenged you to level up and tap back into your unique and divine self? Remember, every piece of your reality is an interpretation. Those can change no matter where you are in this journey.

Chapter 2 – Reuniting With Self-Love

Self-love was a concept so foreign to me until just a few years ago that I cringed anytime the term came up. Why? Because if my father didn't provide me with love and connection, how on earth could I possibly allow myself to feel this for myself? His was the love I craved the most, but I thought it was only given to me if I earned it in some way. That changed once my healing journey over anxiety was well on its way, and I was able to question who I was and what I deserved. Anxiety almost led me to my breaking point—a very well-planned-out suicide attempt that was only withdrawn because of my newborn child. Anxiety also led me to where I am today, to inner peace and the opportunity to change people's lives for the better. What a swing of events. From one extreme to the other in just a few short years. From self-hatred to self-love, from bewilderment to clarity, and from trying to knowing. When I mention going from trying to knowing, I'm referring to my half-hearted attempts to heal anxiety due to the limits and lack of faith I unconsciously put on myself. When mentioning knowing, I'm referring to trusting in my heart's voice to lead me in my decision making and acting swiftly on that knowing.

As Morpheus says in the movie *The Matrix* in his fighting session with Neo, "Stop *trying* to hit me and *hit* me!" There's no better example of trying vs. knowing than this scene.

Oh, how anxiety makes us believers in such illusions—illusions that only bring us more inner distress, which leads to such similarities in the physical world. A person's outer world is just a reflection of their inner world, not at a conscious level, of course. Otherwise, the thousands of daily affirmations in front of the mirror would lead to having all we ever wanted. I'm referring to the subconscious inner world. This infinite storage system has recorded every event in the timeline of a person's life and holds preference with the more intense emotional experiences. These emotionally intense experiences (good or bad) are at the forefront of our perceptual filters, ready to turn what it believes is true into action before we even fully comprehend what's really taking place.

Self-love is ruined by the subconscious mind and its sneaky ways of getting us to identify more and more with what it deems is best for us, which is further pain. Not physical pain, of course. That comes much later on in life if the traumatic zip files held in the body aren't emotionally expressed and resolved. I'm talking about emotional pain without the ability to comprehend the spiritual side of living whatsoever. The subconscious only knows pain based on the one initial sensitizing event that started the snowball toward subsequent events later on in our lives. A good example of these inner workings connected to pain and suffering can be seen in those who date the same type of people again and again—the ones who treat them with little respect. We all know someone in this situation. The moment this person has a real shot at love and is temporarily met with someone respectful and loving, the one addicted to suffering finds a way to destroy the relationship. It's amazing how we can then rationalize why we do what we do (in this case, "he or she wasn't the right type" is a common response) only to find that this rationalization is nothing more than a lie, a trick by the subconscious to pull us back into the painful and familiar.

The incredible thing is that the subconscious mind loves you unconditionally. You heard me right!

It just doesn't look upon change very well. It would rather be stuck in a familiar past (trauma) than take a chance on an unfamiliar future (creation). The reunification with self-love is only achieved when the conscious mind and the subconscious mind work as one. When our thoughts match how we feel, this is a good start. Let me give you an example of this:

Take a moment to say these words to yourself now … "*I make 2 million dollars every year*." What just happened? Well, what happened was you had a moment where you thought, *Boy, that would be nice and my life would change for the better* (thought), followed by a feeling (which always shows up in a part of the body) that made you feel kind of icky. That icky feeling is a reflection of your core beliefs, the part of you that runs the show, and which says you don't deserve it, or it will never happen. Welcome to the world of conscious thought vs. core beliefs, the conscious vs. the subconscious mind.

Beyond anxiety (post anxiety disorder), a person begins aligning their thoughts and core beliefs (ideas and feelings) because their past is no longer deciding their future. Self-love no longer needs to be earned or is something that shows up temporarily after purchasing the newest trending shoes on the market. Instead, self-love is a daily way of living that is reflected in everything a person says and does. Can a person be sucked back into a world of anxiety after having healed through consistent reframing and responding sessions? (This is explained deeply in my second book *F*ck Coping Start Healing*.) It depends on the individual, but it's certainly possible. It can occur in some people who still have deep connections to who they once were and who they've consistently been. Their body's addiction to the stress chemicals that arise when mobilized for a potential threat can show up at any time if their subconscious mind detects a fragment of a past trauma within the present physical reality. A vision, a sound, the texture of something, a smell (the fastest pathway to negative and positive emotions), and even the taste of something may trigger a host of uncomfortable sensations. If allowed to snowball into even deeper anxious emotions, which lead to certain behaviors, there's no telling what direction the person can go in. But, it's more likely that this won't occur due to the perfected art of responding (rather than reacting) to unnecessary stress chemicals as they arise. When a person is beyond anxiety, they know what kind of response leads them where, and they choose wisely at that moment so that a feeling does not turn into an uncontrollable emotion.

Beyond anxiety, self-love isn't within us only during the pleasant moments of life. It's with us during the difficult ones as well.

The byproduct of unconditional self-love is compassion. Being compassionate toward your body in a moment of irrational fear and letting it know of your thanks for preparing you for a threat. Imagine that. Loving what you once hated and wished would never arise again. That's true freedom if you ask me. The result of continued compassion toward ourselves, no matter what the feeling or mistake we believe we may have made, is positive momentum. This is the type of momentum you want to have, not the kind where you're swimming in helplessness because you won't allow yourself the opportunity to see beyond an anxious symptom. No, this kind of momentum unites the conscious and subconscious mind, which places new, loving interpretations over past events and the unknown future.

Beyond anxiety, we are reunited with self-love, and this begins affecting our cells and organ systems more than we know. I'm a big believer in the idea that every single plan to heal someone in any which way must involve the emotional body. Yes, we can improve the mental body, but not be able to effectively bypass the critical factor (the security guard that protects the subconscious beliefs of a person), hence the years of talk therapy that for most people doesn't lead to any long-term emotional or perceptual shifts. Yes, we can look to improve the physical body by dieting or surgically removing a body part that needs removing; however, the question should be what led to the rapid weight gain and the physical illness in the first place? You guessed it; the state of your subconscious mind and your emotional body dictates everything. We'll be going deeper into these aspects later in the book, but for now, understand that the emotional body dictates the state of the physical and energetic body and the experiences you have in the outer world.

As one of my mentors, Brent Baum, mentions: "The overweight person is dieting the wrong body!"

Self-love many times is a result, not a starting point. It's challenging to sit where you are right now and decide that you're going to fall in love with every aspect of you just like that because most of the time, it won't last. Sometimes, the emotions that come with the decision break down the walls of inner resistance. But most of the time, self-love is a result of self-care and prioritizing what is needed for a person to forgive themselves and others so that anger, shame, blame, hate, fear, etc., can be released.

There can be no self-love without forgiveness, period.

During my healing journey, I remember doing chair therapy with my eyes closed and screaming at the chair. On top of the chair was a shirt, which was my dad's, and the smell created an immediate emotional association. I was losing my voice, but I continued screaming. I cried and even kicked the chair at times. Sometimes imaginatively getting justice is what a person needs in order to forgive. In the end, I felt forgiveness toward him and myself as well. Forgiveness for him because the emotional discharge led me to see that he was doing the best he could with what he knew, and his emotionally and physically abusive nature was to motivate me to become a professional athlete. I felt lighter than I ever had before. I didn't just logically forgive; I felt forgiveness in my heart for him and myself, knowing I hadn't done anything wrong. What freedom! What a moment. What possibility for the future. I remember feeling exuberant energy rising up within me like a phoenix from the ashes. That one experience revealed to me the power of our imaginations coupled with emotion to reframe our pasts and let go of old, outdated beliefs.

After months of targeted self-care, I realized how important it was to commit to the potentially messy journey of healing anxiety. I found myself no longer entertaining my old self-hypnotizing ideas based around irrational fear, catastrophic thinking, and mind-reading. I was in a new trance now, one where mistakes didn't exist and setbacks were inevitable learning opportunities for the future. When you are beyond anxiety, you no longer care how many likes your post gets or who comments on it, nor do you look to be complimented for your looks or something you may have done. Your new inner dialogue and compassion for yourself are all you need. The right people begin coming into your life, and strangers start talking to you out of the blue. You begin oozing an energy that others want to be around because we are emotional creatures at our core. Whatever emotional state we bring to each moment sets in motion experiences that further these emotions. Your emotions are like tiny creatures looking to survive as long as they can.

Anxiety will seek experiences that fuel more anxiety, and self-love will seek experiences that fuel more self-love.

Ultimately, how you see yourself and the world comes down to your ability to control your state, and the fastest way to control a person's state is through their body.

Shift your posture to bring about a feeling of empowerment and achievement and hold it for at least 2 minutes. The thoughts you pay attention to will be affected simply through a shift in posture. Now slow down whatever you're doing as well since speed dictates to your nervous system whether the environment (and everything in it) is safe or threatening. Let me say that again.

Your speed dictates safety or threat.

Eat slower, drive slower, talk slower, shower slower, walk slower, and even have sex slower. Become attuned to this slower pace as you notice how your breathing patterns begin to match your speed. When a person is beyond anxiety, these are the kinds of habits that have become their lifestyle. Not something to do to rid ourselves of an anxiety symptom prior to going back to what habits furthered anxiety in the first place. When physical speed is controlled, we have access to the thinking parts of our brain. When physical speed is dictated by the environment and situation, we no longer have the ability to place the meaning we want to over the present moment. Speed is everything. During life after anxiety, there is no longer a conscious focus around speed because it has become automated. A "flow state" is present, one that feels like it couldn't be broken no matter what.

Self-Respect

The days of self-sabotage are over or are coming to an end when we are beyond anxiety. Self-respect is not an ego-based movement. Instead, it comes from our uncorrupted child side that we're now reconnecting with. We came to this world as a blank slate—curious and ready to experience life and all its wonders. Then, as we progressed through the years, we slowly began seeing ourselves in less of an enlightened manner and more so as a problem. Shame is the lowest vibration there is on the consciousness scale. It diminishes a person's self-respect faster than anything else. Soon enough, the person begins prioritizing safety over spontaneity, and all sense of childlike wonder starts fading along with their self-respect.

Life begins open-minded and open-heartedly, then transitions toward living as a mold of our authority figures and how society would like us to be, and then there's the afterlife.

The afterlife isn't life after death so much as it's trading one life for another.

We trade in one life for another. We separate ourselves from our old programming and allow ourselves the opportunity to become enlightened beings each and every day. The afterlife connects you back with the heart-led way of living combined with the experiences gained from the adult mind over the years to create a masterpiece of a human being. Self-respect is no longer something to derive from "doing," but something that is always present based upon simply being. It is no longer seen as something that must be received by others by doing good deeds or through materialism. Rather, self-respect is a genuine sense of self-love over having survived and thrived because of the past. Beyond anxiety, we are grateful for the emotional scars we carry with us, but we no longer allow ourselves to be weighed down by them. There is a sense of peace now whenever our past traumas are brought to our awareness. We no longer feel the need to do anything about them since resolve has already been accomplished at an emotional level.

Beyond anxiety, we are no greater or worse than anyone or anything else.

Those labels no longer exist. Our new identities seem to be connected to a state of positive emptiness now. This is a freeing and incredibly self-loving place, and yet it can never be properly explained to someone who hasn't experienced the afterlife yet. Heck, if you try to understand this place I call positive emptiness further, you will only be depleting your mental and emotional reserves, and you may experience emotional bankruptcy again. Rather, it's meant to be embraced and respected as is. It's a gray area that you can fill with whatever ideas you want to turn into beliefs, whatever actions or inactions you want to connect to your identity, and whatever words you want to live by.

Too often, we overthink something that we don't understand, which brings us full circle back to the original question. That opens up a whole new batch of unanswerable questions that give us something to occupy our time but keeps us stagnant. Put the original question aside. In my transition out of anxiety and into inner peace, I've learned the importance of trusting in that which cannot be answered. If the stars align and an epiphany arises that helps me understand this question better, then great. But if not, life goes on.

This is the kind of trust in life that leads to great levels of self-respect and self-love. I can promise you one thing though, if you choose to live this way forever, you will confuse many people. People hold intelligence at the highest point of value for a person these days, but it has the potential of actually being the lowest. I used to look for answers to everything, hoping that I wouldn't see myself as stupid, or worse, have others see me as stupid. I used to make things up in the moment while gathering up all the will within me so that others agreed with my silly answers.

So much effort. So much discomfort. So much suffering.

Instead, I remember three words that I repeatedly began using that brought a sense of vulnerability and freedom to my life. The words were, *I don't know*. When the topic of politics came up, I spoke less, and when asked what I thought, I would respond with, "I don't know." Many other topics created the same behavioral and verbal reaction from me, which led me to realize that I was truly on the right path toward healing anxiety and no longer looking to prioritize anything else but me until I was fully healthy in every way again. No longer did I grade myself in social settings to see how I did each time. I began respecting myself at a level that was so freeing no matter what I said or did. So let these teachings inspire you to become truly authentic and filled with self-respect again.

The energetic rewards of self-love

Within the consciousness chart presented to us by Dr. David R. Hawkins, we clearly see that love is the beginning of what is referred to on the chart as being "expanded" and within a state of "flow." It is fourth from the top, with the emotions of joy, peace, and enlightenment taking over the top three places. This is an important point to understand as we begin understanding what life is lived like beyond anxiety. Love is a starting point of all great things. Just below love, there is the emotion of reason; this is still a place of understanding more deeply what is to come. Within reason, a person is starting to understand how simple life can be and is beginning to trust the voice of their heart once again. The transition continues beyond reason and into love—a feeling of letting go arises not only in the physical sense but in a mental sense as well. This is because many of the previous ideas that used to create such fear are creating disinterest at this point of self-growth. There is no longer negative momentum being built up through the feelings in the body that attach to the ideas in the mind.

When love arises, there is a sense of loss but also a sense of great inner progress being made.

Energetically, we can conclude through the consciousness chart that love naturally becomes joy, which naturally becomes peace, which naturally meets with enlightenment. But weren't we told all along our artificial lives that joy exists only outside of us? Through the acceptance of others? Through a task that needs to be accomplished? Through an exciting event or product? The digital age of information overload is beginning to lose its power over people because we are beginning to ask better questions of ourselves and life. We used to ask questions like, *How can I be happy?* Now, we're beginning to ask questions like, *What do I truly admire, respect, and love about myself?* Life is starting to become more about the individual and less about others. In turn, the amount of self-care that's shown is beginning to unconsciously affect others and the world as a whole.

Love leads to joy.
Joy leads to peace.
Peace leads to enlightenment.

Let me tell you an honest truth. I couldn't stand myself for many years. Not so much on the surface, but at a deeper level. I hated how I had failed at what I set to accomplish. Later, I realized that what I had set to accomplish didn't come from my heart but was only for the sake of others. I also hated how I relied on other people and "miraculous" self-help techniques to end my anxiety. Only later did I realize that a big part of me wasn't ready to let go of the suffering and pain. This is an important note because love can only arise once focus is turned from what you might lose to what you will gain. We naturally focus on worst-case scenarios out of safety by the reptilian brain to maintain our social status and physical survival. No one wants to be ostracized by a group because that would signal death to the primitive brain. So we do whatever it takes to maintain our lives the way they are. Change, even good change, is a threat because we can't see beyond the first few steps in the journey.

Healing arises when we *expect* healing to arise.

This expectation is not hope; it's intent. If there isn't a clear intention, there is no change, and if there is no change, you will survive but never thrive. Beyond anxiety, we are love. During anxiety, we are fear (most of it irrational fear, in fact). There is no one healthy food that can override an emotionally unhealthy person. Nor is there one unhealthy food that can override an emotionally healthy being. In an energetic sense, love is the greatest force that opens the floodgates to things we, in society, don't truly understand yet. In Eastern traditions, people live through their hearts; in the West, they live through their minds. We sense what is right in the West, but we are afraid to reveal and act on it, whereas in the East, there is more purity and less roboticness in general. Eastern traditions and healings are seen as alternative methods of healing in the West, at least on paper. But an awakening is occurring at this moment in the West. People are beginning to see beyond their old programming and opening themselves up to the unfamiliar more. It's a beautiful thing to witness and be a part of.

As love begins to prevail over fear, we are met with the power of the female and male bonding hormones, respectively, oxytocin and vasopressin. These hormones have the potential to over-write past neurologically programmed behaviors and rewrite them in a way that fits with your beautiful journey. The more these hormones get released, the more malleable the system becomes, and the less serious life becomes. This release happens with laughter, which relieves tension, positive human touch, intense pleasure, orgasms, and, at the core of it all, love. Notice how none of these things can be faked, and yet when dealing with anxiety, all of them are. We laugh in social situations to fit in, we move away from human touch, and we deny ourselves pleasure out of guilt and other core beliefs. Beyond anxiety, we open up to it all. We allow ourselves to experience what we once restricted ourselves from, and life gets larger in a sense. When love is present, our perceptual filters pick up optimism and joy. When fear is present, we are more pessimistic and even lifeless at times. During my days living with an anxiety disorder, I felt I no longer had a soul or a spirit anymore. To me, a soul is our connection to source energy, and our spirit is the vibration we emanate from moment to moment. No one deserves to live a life of feeling like they are lifeless.

Lifelessness is another clever way the subconscious mind keeps us from pursuing change.

Why would the deepest parts of us do this, you may ask? To fulfill the beliefs held at the deepest levels within us because the subconscious mind-body cannot differentiate between good and bad. It only seeks to maintain what came first and is repeated most often. Love is the exit strategy away from a feeling of lifelessness. It gives life. Since you are the co-creator of your life—with God readily beside you—it's up to you to show life where your heart stands. Remember, emotions are the language this universe uses to understand what it is you want more of. So spend only a little time reasoning with yourself, and take the leap to love now.

Summary:

Fear is suffering and getting by, and most people are content with fear. However, love is flow, and that will lead to the ultimate form of consciousness, which is enlightenment. We have more power than we think, but when fear and suffering are so readily present, we cannot see these limitless inner resources. We all have a sense of what the right thing to do is for us to meet with love again. Many of us are afraid of what unknowns may arise if we follow this unfamiliar path that is love, and therein lies the problem. I'd like you to take a few moments right now to notice where it is you're living within the consciousness graph mentioned in this chapter. The purpose of this inner exploration is not to experience a sense of guilt or shame; it's to be honest as to what signals you're sending out to the world. Once you've pinpointed where you are emotionally living from day to day, notice how courage is the major stepping-stone toward a flow state of living and away from suffering. Ask yourself, *What is it that I must be courageous toward? What action am I pushing aside and neglecting that keeps showing up at certain times?* Courage breeds neutrality and a further willingness to be more courageous until it becomes a way of life. Remember this.

Chapter 3 – Welcoming Disconnection and Separation

Beyond anxiety, there is a period when people feel disconnected from others, materialism, and even the physical world itself. They begin feeling this sense of disconnect is a bad thing when it's actually a sign of an inner and outer transition occurring. The need for external validation and stimulation begins lessening until total disinterest arises. This feeling of disconnect is scary at first, confusing in the middle but rewarding in the end. Here's how one of my coaching clients, Shirley, explained her experience of disconnect to me:

Dennis,

I have this feeling of total detachment, and it frightens me while at the same time I can't help but be curious over it. I'm realizing that because of all the self-care work I've put in, this must be a positive thing rather than a negative thing, and yet a small part of me is still questioning what it exactly is. I feel lighter, clearer, and more optimistic than ever in my life, and this disconnect toward the world feels like an awakening of some sort. I'm looking forward to the fears and the excitement over this feeling and can't wait to update you on how things go in the future.

Much love,
Shirley

At this point in her journey, we can clearly see how Shirley can't yet pinpoint what this feeling and experience truly is. You can feel a sense of apprehension and anticipation in her letter as they're both tugging at her to win over her perception of this inner experience. As someone who's gone through such bouts of disconnect and separation from the external, I can tell you from personal experience that it must be fully embraced. The reason being, certain doors are naturally closing, and others are opening. Most people think going beyond anxiety and healing is one straight path. They think that if they do the right things for themselves, life will somehow move all challenges out of the way and only present positives. This sort of perception should only be left for the movies, not true reality.

Often along the healing journey, the more blocks, unhelpful beliefs, and traumas you reframe and move beyond, the more unfamiliar challenges arise.

It's like opening a box with all the missing pieces of information connected to your years of suffering. When disconnect arises, here are some of the common experiences:

- You start losing more and more interest in old friends who used to bring you down into a lower vibration.
- Your desire for more and more money withers away, and you become more grateful for the miracles you already have in your life.
- You find yourself wanting to be more playful again, like a child.

- You're beginning to see beyond your stress and belittling things that used to send you into anxiety.
- You feel a form of depersonalization at a physical level, but you can sense that it's different from the emotional weight you used to carry within.

These are just a few of the many occurrences that happen when a person meets with disconnection along the healing path. There also tends to be a disconnect from stagnancy around your career. You begin viewing your career through the eyes of a more enlightened being and sense that there are better things to do with that much time. The feeling of disconnection while on the healing path is a gateway to a person's true purpose and mission in life. This calling is brought to you; it's not something you think up. As life opens its doors to you to experience it fully, we have choices to make. Either we embrace the vulnerability of change, or we go back to staying stuck. We must choose at this point to continue on our healing path doing what we've never done before, stepping out of our comfort zones, and gathering further wisdom along the way.

Be a "Yes Man," or woman!

Of course, you don't have to be as extreme as Jim Carrey's character in the movie *Yes Man*, but it's a similar idea. Remember when we noted the consciousness chart in the last chapter; the progression from suffering to a flow state begins with courage right there in the middle. The thing about courage is that you only need a few seconds or a few minutes of it; after that, the signal of safety is sent to your nervous system.

The longer you spend doing something, the faster your perceptual filters change, and your body gets the signal that it doesn't need to mobilize itself through stress hormones to run or fight back.

In this sense, time does heal, but not before action is taken.

This form of disconnection is positive, and it's not so much physical as it is emotional and spiritual. After years of helping anxiety sufferers, I'm convinced that this is far less a mental-health problem and far more a spiritual-health problem. When trauma occurs, our spirit suffers, and we lose parts of our true selves, our soul. As we heal our traumas through reframing practices (visit my YouTube channel and theanxietyguy.com for more information on reframing) and proper self-care, we regain those soul pieces, and our spirit thrives. We go from feeling lifeless to full of life with plenty of inner and outer "messiness" in between.

Let's dive a little deeper into disconnection and what to expect when going beyond anxiety.

Mental Disconnection

During mental disconnection, the fearful thoughts that once sent you into an inner frenzy are lessened in frequency and strength. Those fearful thoughts are still there because the subconscious mind's job is to keep you safe, but the world is beginning to look safer and less threatening. At this deep level of shifts in perceptual filters, a person feels like life is giving them a second chance to "get it right." The years spent learning the ropes of what life is and staying within the boundaries set by society begin losing their pull. The interesting part of this period of awakening is what's possible, rather than what we must do to keep things the same.

During mental disconnection, we think less and be more.

There is no longer a pull toward overthinking, which opens up the voice of the intuition, the heart's voice. We make mistakes, and yet they don't feel like mistakes, just life. As our intuition grows, we sense things in other people more easily. We are beginning to tap into what we lost along the way, such as our psychic abilities and sensitivities. This is a different kind of sensitivity. Not the kind we experienced over the years while dealing with anxiety. Rather, this level of sensitivity goes deeper than maintaining our survival. We are sensitive to the trees listening to what we say about them, and the animals looking to interact playfully with us. Life becomes more about experiencing and less about surviving.

Emotional Disconnection

At the level of emotional disconnection, good feelings often turn into good emotions, but bad feelings rarely do. An involuntary bodily reaction connected with feeling arises, but there is a wall that gets in the way of its negative progress. With emotional disconnection, good feelings take priority, and we no longer feel like we are forcing these feelings. You may find yourself embarking on a life of service work, such as life coaching, and it feels natural. This sort of endeavor brings newfound meaning to your life. You find that while helping another, you feel less emotional toward their story. This can be interpreted as being insensitive or simply the state you need to be in to help others. When we allow our feelings to turn into emotions, we lose our ability to think at that moment. As we emotionally mature, we find ourselves in just the right state to help another while simultaneously helping ourselves through the wisdom we are repeatedly gaining.

Emotional disconnection is letting go of the old and bringing in the new.

Here's a story that will help you to understand emotional disconnection better.

A few years ago, one of my uncles passed away. When this happened, I had an initial moment of shock followed by a sense of peace. That sense of peace was connected to everything that my uncle had taught me and the experiences we had shared. I felt that he had lived a full life, and for that, I was happy. These days, many people look to live a long life rather than a satisfying one, and I believe this can be questioned. My family grew concerned about my non-reaction to his death; they didn't understand my perspectives very well. I, however, had a heart sense that his soul was in a good place, and the long-term grief would be unnecessary from my own perceptions along with his. You always have a choice—to focus on the life of someone or the loss. Our choices determine the level of emotional maturity we exude, which ultimately determines our happiness.

Behavioral Disconnection

At the behavioral level, we understand that time is the most precious thing, so we do what is important for our souls and the betterment of the world. We recognize how many of the things we did in the past held little-to-no meaning, and meaning is what we begin gravitating toward. We behave the way we want to, we talk with purpose and don't enjoy small talk as much, and we see fear as an opportunity to grow. Because we see fear as an opportunity for emotional maturity, we welcome it and move toward it. The experience strengthens our resolve over meeting with inner peace and enlightenment.

To behave as someone wants you to is to suffer; to behave in a way that feels natural is to live.

That natural way of behaving from moment to moment comes with a feeling of "putting yourself out there." It's a vulnerable feeling. It's like starting a new sport—you have no clue how it's going to go. The beauty is that the more time you spend with that vulnerable feeling, the less vulnerable you will feel. You begin feeling certain, not just confident, but certain, and it makes you want to take on new situations in a similar manner. The biggest problem I see in today's mental-health treatments is how we separate out all these different parts of healing rather than understanding the very thing that naturally leads to them falling into place—love. Everything we do, good or bad, is out of and for love. The vast majority of anxiety sufferers today don't know it or won't admit it, but they are unconsciously keeping their anxiety identities alive in the hope of feeling the love they never received when they were young. These are known as secondary gains, things we do to gain something we never had (beginning at childhood, onward). No one wants to suffer. But the truth is that the non-suffering never brought forth the love needed, so the subconscious will do everything in its power to have its needs met; therefore, anxiety survives. Is this the case for all anxiety sufferers? No. But through this journey of self-care and self-love, you begin learning things about yourself that you might have a hard time admitting to yourself and others. You can't heal without being honest with yourself and recognizing the core reasons why you do what you do. This truly is the most freeing place.

Ultimately, this period of separation and disconnection is a positive thing that must be fully accepted as part of a deeper transition.

This transition takes you beyond yourself and into a much larger world. No longer do you focus solely on your own problems. Instead, you begin recognizing the burdens that each of us carries and how a corrupt world system has drowned out the life and soul of so many individuals. Intuitively, you are growing stronger. You feel that you are beginning to understand rather than trying, commit rather than dabbling, and act rather than overthinking. As you welcome this positive separation and disconnection, what used to feel like sacrifices will not feel like sacrifices as much anymore. This process will lead you toward becoming more curious as to what you're moving toward.

Summary:

We now understand that the feeling of disconnection and separation is a transitional period that must be respected and followed, not internalized as something wrong with us. Often, we initially sense that any change that arises without our intent or action is bad or wrong in some way. As we allow ourselves to see these changes in a neutral and more nonjudgmental manner, we allow them to accompany us and teach us what we need to learn about ourselves in order to take those next steps toward true inner peace and fulfillment. Remember, life is always looking to work for you, not against you. The feeling of disconnection holds within it lessons that will lead you toward a newfound connection with all that is within life. The feeling of separation from others will only bring you both closer toward each other in the future, should this be the way it's meant to be for you both. Remember, nothing is either good or bad; it's your perceptions that make it so. So choose to perceive this chapter of disconnection and separation in a way that leads to continued inner growth and unconditional love for life.

Chapter 4 – From Being Led to Leading: Creation Rather than Stagnation

As we begin identifying the world that is upon us beyond living with an anxiety disorder, we begin recognizing the non-forcefulness that comes upon us. We're starting to feel a sense of gentleness toward ourselves and every living creature. This gentleness comes with a sense that we can welcome the uncertainties of life rather than forcefully trying to understand each aspect of it, which leaves us feeling even more tired and wired.

During anxiety, we are led without knowing we are being led.

Our parents' feelings have unconsciously become our own feelings. We unconsciously hold on to these feelings until we can consistently tap into the courage to allow these exact feelings to dissipate, and we can come into our own.

We must truly understand that the civil war taking place within us (between the knowledgeable adult mind and the emotional child-mind) is at play every moment of the day.

The child-mind (subconscious) would much rather lead the way in terms of perceptions and actions, since leaving this up to the more-experienced adult mind would potentially lead to more failures, even potential death. The adult mind sees beyond these irrational ideas but can never fully convince the subconscious child-mind to adopt a new way of approaching reality. That is until emotion and consistency overtake stagnancy and fear. A train running at full speed has an exceedingly difficult time stopping suddenly. The train has gathered a tremendous amount of momentum and gains more speed as it moves forward toward a dedicated destination. The same occurs for the person who has found themselves and is ready to lead rather than be led. This person is growing tired of living without purpose as dissatisfaction overtakes the stagnancy of comfortable discomfort.

To lead others may or may not be a conscious choice.

Sometimes we decide that our past struggles, which led us to tremendous clarity, may hold value for others, so we may choose to lead others toward a similar outcome. Other times, we are led toward a teacher status by an intelligence inside that we might not fully understand and might never understand. We all have leadership potential within us, but we must have first gone through the darkness ourselves to truly lead and inspire. Those who have are the best teachers/healers. As rapport is built between the newly active teacher and the student (in this case, the present anxiety sufferer), half the battle is already won. When a sufferer feels understood, they are much more likely to accept suggestions from the teacher. If, however, the sufferer or student feels misunderstood, there is no amount of time or wisdom from the teacher that can alter the mental and emotional state of the sufferer. Out there in the vast ocean of self-help teachers, there are also the highly motivational ones who spur on a dopamine rush with every word they preach. Bless them for wanting to make a difference in other peoples' lives. Many are genuine; however, as much as the adrenaline rush temporarily eliminates feelings of anxiety, the symptoms will come back again. This can become an emotional roller coaster. The addiction to the surge of motivation and adrenaline feels helpful, even euphoric at times. But there is no direction, no clear intent, no plan; therefore, it will fail in the end.

Remember: Anxiety recovery is just the beginning.

It is not an end to achieve, not a finish line of some sort, but rather a fresh start. Whenever we start something new, we must continue to grow our inner and outer peace in order to maintain our progress. This is why it's important to understand that the leader, or in this case, the person healing from anxiety leading others, must continue to grow as well. Just because the teacher has more moments of mental and emotional neutrality doesn't mean they have all they need to guide another person. If the teacher doesn't grow, the student won't grow either. The teacher is attempting to show the anxiety sufferer a life filled with creation rather than a life solely focused on prevention. Preventing the worst from happening comes from the reptilian part of the brain that's connected to our primal drives. When the emotional brain or limbic system accompanies the survival brain, we begin believing in threats that don't even exist. It acts like a mirage placed over our senses leading us toward a life that is small and yet comfortably uncomfortable. The teacher, or leader, takes the mirage away and reveals the truth behind the situation or environment to the sufferer. This allows the sufferer to once and for all make their own conscious decisions about their past and future.

A life of prevention is a life of stagnation.

To live such a stuck and anxious life sucks the creativity and zest out of a person. Not only this, but an anxiety sufferer no longer is clear on how to act, when to allow emotions to arise, and even how to verbalize their thoughts. The teacher takes the confusion out of the picture by showing them the path toward higher consciousness. This place of higher consciousness is a step-by-step process. We might not even be aware of this as we embark on the transformation, which looks like the following:

The Start: Negative states (fear, anger, disgust, sadness, blame, guilt).

The Becoming: Balance (neutrality, understanding, respect for self and others, intuition strengthening, compassion, inner healing).

The Truth: Rebirth (deep awakening, true love, energy over matter, flow state, leadership qualities, no more good and bad but only life itself).

You can see how we become much less consciously and unconsciously judgmental and much more accepting of anything and everything. As we are led toward leading others, we are simultaneously becoming no one and everyone. We no longer feel identified with our careers, our past, even our parents. We are pure love and energy, vibrating this love and energy into the world. At the same time, we feel deeply connected to everything around us, human or not. Our relationships seem to be blossoming with a tenth of the effort we had put into it while we were suffering from anxiety. Often, more effort will only give you the opposite of what you desire. This must be recognized quickly in our own lives.

Can the trees hear what I think and say?

I remember taking a walk in nature one day and coming across one particular tree that stood out to me. I sat down on the bench in front of it, looking to understand this tree better and how it had grabbed my attention. As I sat down, I looked at the center of the bench only to see the words *The trees can hear*. Back in the days of my addiction to suffering, I would have ridiculed these words, but I was on a transformational path and was open to understanding what these words meant to me. At that moment, I remembered the rice experiment done by Japanese professor Masaru Emoto where he prepared three jars of rice with enough water to submerge the rice. These were separated by labels on each. This was an experiment based on the claim that human consciousness could affect the molecular structure of water.

> Label 1 read, "I love you."
> Label 2 read, "You idiot."
> He completely ignored the third jar.

After a month, the rice that was cognitively "thanked" was fermented and had a pleasant smell. The rice that was affronted turned black. The rice that was ignored began to rot. Could this mean that our intentions, thoughts, feelings, and emotions can directly affect everything outside of us? I personally believe this to be the case without a doubt.

As I looked back on this powerful and vibrant tree, I felt a deeper connection with it. I began thinking thoughts of connection and wanted to take a particular lesson from my beautiful encounter that day, so I placed an intention toward it. In those moments, I knew the importance of allowing the lesson to come to me rather than overthinking it into reality. Overthinking is a defense mechanism that anxiety sufferers revert to when they feel confused and threatened. This is a very tricky act that the inner child implements in order for us to become less trusting in our intuition, just in case it leads us astray again (as it did for many of us during our childhood before becoming cognitively active). The interesting thing about intention is that the more emotion behind the intention, the more likely it will manifest. Intending something to arise without emotion is like using a computer without a keyboard. The main signal that gets sent to the subconscious mind—that something is vitally important to you and is more of a need than a want—is the emotional intent that accompanies the cognitive one. I knew my lesson from my encounter with that tree would arise soon, as the voice rang loud within me:

“Stand effortlessly no matter what.”

My interpretation of this vital lesson was that a tree may lose its branches, and the leaves may fall off, but the tree itself is unmoved. It does not fret over what we would deem as a loss for the tree. Rather, the tree embraces the never-ending changes that come from being a tree. At the level of suffering from anxiety, our thoughts and beliefs come solely from manmade creations around what to fear. In reality, the very ideas and feelings that send us into an anxious state are not ours but someone else's. They are a byproduct of the bombardment of advertising around fear we unconsciously recognize daily and are connected to traumatic experiences from our past that hold little-to-no truth within them. As teachers and students of anxiety, we must welcome each and every new chapter in our lives with open arms, just as the tree does. We must learn to be open to different experiences and respect the ever-changing process of personal growth.

The most uncomfortable and potentially painful thing you will ever have to do in your life is heal an anxiety disorder. It is by far the most rewarding act, as well.

It's a very new thing to us when we encounter creation over stagnation. For many years, we stayed stuck in a rarely fulfilling job because of the security of a paycheck, only to see the slavery in that and the time lost. For many years, we kept our negative relationships with others alive due to being already connected to them only to see that our separation from them would lead to the very best thing they and we needed. We live stagnated lives out of a desire for comfort, the need for a sense of certainty, and because it's familiar. At least until we've suffered enough. This moment could arise at any age, but it always arises. The question is what is done when it arises. Some talk themselves out of moving toward creation by thinking about all the consequences rather than the benefits of this change. We justify living a stagnant life because of what others may think of us and because we've connected many parts of it to who we believe we are. The inner child is very opportunistic, as we've mentioned before. Its goal is safety, and these ideas are nothing more than defense mechanisms toward keeping things as they've always been.

Former anxiety sufferers who now lead others understand that the ideas coming from the inner child must be respected but no longer need to be accepted.

The last thing you wanted when you were a child was to be hated, ostracized from a group, disconnected, or unloved, so I ask you why you continue to be so critical of these ideas coming from your own inner child? Hasn't he or she suffered enough? Isn't it time to work with your inner child rather than continue to allow it to believe things about themselves and this world that are false at best? Your initial feelings are beliefs—in fact, core beliefs running at the level of your subconscious mind. Even if your conscious beliefs change, but your core beliefs stay the same, your life will not change one bit. This is where the rebuilding of the relationship between your adult mind and your child-mind will blossom into a beautiful coherence between your conscious and unconscious or core beliefs. This is when your desires will be fulfilled toward your own health along with your external reality. This is when effortless living brings about fruitful results. There is no forcing anymore; we no longer contaminate the energy and frequency we put out into the world through these two opposing belief systems. They become as one. When unwanted ideas or feelings arise, we are guiding rather than looking to distract ourselves. We no longer feel a desire to stuff aside what we don't want to feel or think by turning up the volume of a song in our car. Rather, we are beginning to treat our inner child and its old beliefs similar to the compassion and understanding we have toward our own children's fears and beliefs. The result is a blissful life experience.

Summary:

Life has an interesting way of teaching us what we need to learn in order to live the way we were meant to live. As we naturally become more drawn toward creating our own set of core beliefs that mirror that of our conscious beliefs, we will be met with many defense mechanisms that look to keep us in a stagnant life. Everything changes, and we must change with it. Even dying is a transition from one form to another, one existence to another, as the spirit succeeds the human body. We came to this world as creative and unique beings only to believe that our creativity won't ever be met with loving arms, and our uniqueness is less valuable than what is already here within others. To lead is to lead by action, more so than any other way. When we act in accordance with who we are working toward becoming, we are not only once and for all living true to ourselves but also true to others. Our words then have meaning. We are in love with depth in every way rather than succumbing to surface-level stuff. Life begins guiding us rather than us looking to guide life. Remember, you are in communication with all that is in this world at every moment of every day. Make sure you are communicating the message that life can be a wonderful journey rather than a long dark tunnel with no end in sight.

Chapter 5 – Cooperation Replaces Competition

Beyond anxiety, we find ourselves moving toward cooperation and away from competition during the continuation of building our newfound identities. This new insight and recognition is often a result of looking beyond competing with others and seeing it as a mindset that leads to division. This world is already very much divided; it is divided in every sense. When we come to this world, our natural tendency is to connect, to find similarities between others and us. As we grow up, this inner need to connect is replaced with a need to divide, to separate from in order to feel a sense of worthiness and even superiority.

Connection is our true nature; division is our learned nature.

To illustrate this reconnection with cooperation beyond anxiety better, I have to go back to my own healing journey. I was tired of fighting, tired of allowing the inner child within me to sort for and find the threat in everything. I realized at the time that we have feelings and emotions, but we are neither our feelings nor our emotions; this is an important distinction. I used to think that my feelings were truth. These feelings were followed up with justifications from my thinking mind about why someone or some situation truly was a potential threat. These feelings, which were coupled with my thoughts, led me to experience emotions of division and separation and only strengthened these core beliefs within me.

Our inner child is all-loving, all-caring, so much so that it goes above and beyond every chance he or she gets. We begin believing the interpretations and perceptions of the inner child as we drift farther from cooperation during anxiety and closer toward competition. We soon find ourselves competing with everything and everyone in the hope of providing ourselves a glimpse into what it would be like to feel worthy. As we grew up, many of us weren't given the love, connection, and support we truly needed. Instead, we witnessed conflict, constant conflict in our outside world, which led us to believe that life is threatening and that fighting is the only way.

First, we look to cooperate, then we learn to compete, and eventually, we go back to cooperating.

Why? Because we see no value in competing anymore. Beyond anxiety, there is more to life than making more money, climbing the corporate ladder, being a better athlete than someone else, being smarter than others, having more luxuries and toys than your neighbor, etc. We begin realizing how none of these attempts make our world a better place. Some may think that there is a middle ground called friendly competition, but the truth is no competition is friendly until after the competition has ended. At some level, we will do whatever it takes to win the battle, to be better than.

Beyond anxiety, we are naturally brought back toward our earliest childhood years. Our true nature begins shining through once again, and we prefer cooperation in each aspect of life. We even begin realizing that cooperation can get us much farther than competition can. We come back into our own and have a sense that we are in some way purifying this planet. Cooperation not only begins arising with other people. We begin cooperating with nature and, most importantly, our inner child once again. Our initial feelings toward something or someone are now seen as one perceptual option out of many potentials. We come from an understanding place at this point as we move away from being emotionally reactive and toward pleasantly responsive. It's not that we shut out our emotions at this level of being. Rather, we stop allowing our feelings to turn into emotions we no longer want to experience. During anxiety, we fight for the feeling of control; therefore, competition in all aspects rules our life. The less competitive we are, the less control we'll have, or at least that is what it seems when such a deep feeling of sensitivity and anxiety runs a person's life. The interesting thing is that beyond anxiety, during the inner healing process, we give up fighting and control and therefore feel like we have much more of it than we ever had. Isn't that an interesting realization, so interesting that I have to share these words again but in a slightly different way:

Give up the habits that you think provide you with a sense of control over your life to truly be met with real control over your life.

As cooperation replaces competition, we begin living in a place of allowance rather than striving for more and better. During the multiple decades of my life living with anxiety, I would put tremendous pressure on myself to comprehend something I didn't understand in the moment. I would consistently overthink the answer, to the point of such deep guilt for not understanding and such deep blame toward my parents for not preparing me well enough for these types of situations. Beyond anxiety, I realized that overthinking only leads to more questions and rarely ever leads to the right answer, or any answer, for that matter. When we use our cognitive resources at such a strenuous level, we are depleting ourselves and our energy reserves at the deepest levels. By 2 pm, many anxiety sufferers feel like they have nothing more they can give; they are exhausted! Exhaustion leads to self-pity and a victim-like state, and so the cycle turns into an identity. We begin identifying with being a victim. And since this is such a familiar place to live in, we unconsciously reject our own attempts to transition into a new identity. We are half-hearted in our dedication to change, and it's not our fault, but rather a system within us that's meant to work at the highest level of efficiency. The inner child doesn't want to relearn everything about life all over again and alter who it believes it is. It would rather maintain this run of good survival luck by strengthening the current ways it perceives itself and the world, therefore seeing more threats in things that were once neutral.

The inner child will change its beliefs once it recognizes that you genuinely want this change to happen.

The only way for this to arise is through emotion and consistency. When a new feeling about something leads to a compounding effect where you begin thinking, speaking, imagining, and acting in line with a new, more pleasant feeling, it identifies that a new perception is safe to adopt. When this new response is consistently applied over time, the person no longer has to be so conscious about the new response; they are in a state of unconscious competence. The process looks like this:

1) Unconscious incompetence — we don't know that we don't know something about something.
2) Conscious incompetence — we now realize something about something that we didn't before.
3) Conscious competence — we are now beginning to apply what we know to make a change.
4) Unconscious competence — the change is becoming automatic, and our core beliefs are shifting to match our conscious adult-mind beliefs.

You can see how when we are beyond anxiety, moving away from competition and toward cooperation, this process naturally takes shape. For myself, I would have these amazing epiphanies as I went through the day. Epiphanies that my inner child rejected, but my adult mind absolutely appreciated. I realized how much time and effort was being put forward to try and maintain who I thought I was and what I believed. I started becoming more compassionate toward others and more understanding. During my years with anxiety, it was me against them. Beyond anxiety, it is us against no one. There is no enemy; there are only core beliefs led by the inner child based on unpleasant experiences from the past. My compassion toward others led to something I wanted so deeply but could never achieve through willpower and more effort, letting go. Beyond anxiety, when someone succeeds in some endeavor, I no longer feel a sense of jealousy and hatred toward them. I feel appreciation and love. Letting go is something we strive for but never seem to fully grasp and apply in our lives. The reason is because we try to do so. The more beautiful we try to look, the uglier we feel, the more accepted we look to be by others, the more rejected we feel. It's the extra effort that we feel we need to apply to each aspect of our lives that leads to never fully realizing our full potential—to let go and be as we are, as we were meant to be.

Competing is hard; cooperating is easy.

We are not living in the wild, running around the jungle trying to stay alive and competing with all the other animals for food and territory. We are human beings with the capability to consistently cooperate and have all we ever need in this lifetime. Anxiety breeds competition; inner peace breeds cooperation. When anxiety becomes the norm, our perceptual filters change dramatically and constantly. We become storytellers to ourselves, and we begin to believe those stories because of their frequency and the emotion that accompanies them. We start to feel like our anxiety is situational. We tell ourselves it's because of a colleague at work or a critical judgment made by someone, but nothing could be farther from the truth. We turn into pure animals fighting for our lives, our money, and our families. The reason we don't recognize that we are fighting is that it feels normal. The media, advertisers, and our friends all lead us toward believing this. Beyond anxiety, however, we see that same coworker from a point of compassion, and we no longer take things personally.

Taking another person's opinions of you to heart becomes a strange idea to someone beyond anxiety. It just does not make sense.

We feel a natural permission being given to us to allow us to work with life, work with our finances, and our families. Who gives this permission is up for discussion; everyone will have a different opinion. However, my theory is that what we give out, we receive. Not at a cognitive level, not at a behavioral level, not even at a verbal level, but at a feeling and a core-belief level. Our core beliefs are connected to our feelings, our feelings spur on emotions, and our emotions hold the language that this universe reads. Nothing changes permanently on the inside or outside until we have consistent emotional shifts toward life and everything in it. This is also connected to your past since your past is being communicated through your body. Your past is your present; your past is your future. It's not necessarily what happened, but the way you emotionally feel toward what happened. We can talk the talk all day every day, but unless we are emotionally invested in the perceptual changes we think and speak, the universe will continue to read you as wanting more suffering. This addiction to suffering is connected to competition because competition is suffering. There is always someone or something more to compete with. That attitude of competition never allows a person to be in the present, only the future based on beliefs from the past.

When we stop competing and we replace it, we stop suffering.

Cooperating is easy when you are beyond anxiety. It's easy in the sense that it feels effortless now. No longer is anyone prettier or better looking than you because neither exists anymore. Your strict judgments have been replaced with understanding. The understanding that "better" means nothing in the big picture. We are all one, and we are all mirrors of one another in one way or another; past, present, or future. That is why seeing someone as ugly means seeing yourself as ugly, which no longer occurs beyond anxiety because physical ugliness no longer exists. Of course, we still recognize the internal pressures in others, but we don't separate from them or distance ourselves from them anymore. Our simply being in the presence of someone for long enough periods allows them to tap into more choices on how to be, who to be, and how to respond to life.

No one loses when we cooperate, everyone loses when we compete.

As cooperation becomes the guide to living life fruitfully, we begin seeing how wrong our old core and conscious beliefs truly were. We recognize that although these beliefs kept us in a perpetual state of suffering, we do not feel a sense of wasted time. Rather, we are brought toward gratitude for having the experience of anxiety in our lives. Gratitude for anxiety, imagine that. Tell that to any anxiety sufferer who is struggling today, and you may get a black eye. You simply cannot comprehend what you can finally comprehend when you are beyond anxiety. Therefore, healing anxiety is a step-by-step process, and many times we don't even consciously recognize the steps we're taking to heal because they are a natural byproduct of the wisdom we are gaining along the way.

But competition is everywhere these days, isn't it? It's even in places you don't think it exists, like retail stores. Why do people buy better and better clothing and the latest mainstream brands? Because it makes them temporarily feel better about themselves while feeling above others who don't wear what they do. "But clothes make me feel put together," one may say. These words are nothing more than a rationalization based on a low level of self-worth and self-respect. When you own these things, which are available to you beyond anxiety and during the transition to cooperation, every piece of clothing looks the same to you. There is no difference anywhere.

This applies to more than clothing. You no longer have a favorite sports team, a favorite meal, a favorite friend, etc. Because you no longer live in a world of separation between good and bad. Instead, you live in a world where everything is connected. You watch sports and feel neutral toward the game. You eat a meal and are pleasantly enjoying it without judgment comparing this and that. And your best friend is no longer a best friend, but rather a friend, maybe a very close one, but there is no longer a clinging onto them because you are now open to the unfamiliar. The unfamiliar in this case is the ability to grow your relationship circle. People often label someone as being their "best friend" out of a fear of loss. Beyond anxiety, there is no best, and there is no worst because we are beginning to see beyond matter, beyond things. We are opening up to an energetic world governed by universal laws that are always in effect. When you can understand and make use of these laws, you begin finding yourself connected and in harmony with all that is in this world. The laws are:

1) The Law of Vibration — This is just another way of talking about the law of attraction, which many people today are familiar with. Everything has a vibration. When we are competition-focused, we give and receive information; likewise, when we are cooperating. This information brings forth more feelings and experiences connected to it, which makes our abilities to not allow negative feelings to turn into steady negative emotions that much more important.
2) The Law of Relativity — Everything is relative to something else. A gigantic problem to one

person may be a piece of cake for another. When we are hyper-focused on something, it grows in strength and importance, which can lead to overwhelm. One of the best things I ever did to end the cycle of making things worse was to see the situation from the angle of an outside security camera or a bystander. My perspective was flawed; however, the perspective of a neutral observer held the potential to become less reactive and more responsive.

3) The Law of Cause and Effect — Most of the things you have created in your life originated from an unconscious place, but you still ultimately created the reality you live in today. Everything has a beginning, a middle, and an end. This is the law of cause and effect. When we are beyond anxiety and transitioning away from competition, and toward cooperation, there is also a progression. There are temptations to once again compete when a strong desire to become something more or better arises. The beauty is that the greater our awareness becomes, the faster we can recognize when we're headed down a path we no longer want and change the course of our lives.
4) The Law of Polarity — Everything has an opposite side. You can't have up without down, left without right, masculine without feminine. In the anxiety world, we recognize the starting point to healing here; if there is suffering, there must also be freedom. Hope is a great starting point but an awful main strategy for healing. Remember that.

5) The Law of Gestation — Gestation is the period it takes for something to come into form. Just as a baby goes through a gestation period of nine months, so does the energetic connection to all things take its own time to manifest. Beyond anxiety, we respect this law, we work with it, and we allow natural byproducts of our self-care work to arise in time. We no longer forcefully look for answers or make something happen this instant. Rather, we see life as our friend, our provider, and we allow the right answers and the next steps to come to us intuitively and through our infinite wisdom.
6) The Law of Rhythm — Everything has a rhythm to it. When we are in rhythm, we are in harmony. When we are out of rhythm, we feel it but often don't like to admit it to ourselves. An effortless and peaceful life is within reach for anyone at any stage of their anxiety recovery. However, to tap into this emotional state consistently, one must recognize when they're flying too high or too low in life and bring themselves back into alignment with the natural flow of life. Beyond anxiety, we understand this deeply. During anxiety, however, this may confuse someone. That's OK because there is plenty of confusion until the light at the end of the tunnel brightens.
7) The Law of Transmutation — The transmutation period is when things you are working on arc going haywire, or you're beginning to feel highly uncomfortable. You feel like you should give up, stop, or go back to your familiar past. But like a caterpillar going

> through the messiness of becoming a butterfly, your experience won't be much different. There will be setbacks, and there will be wins on this path toward deeper understanding. The question is, which one will you focus on more?

At this point in the book, I wanted to give you a deeper understanding of the "rules of life," so to speak. We do all sorts of positive and negative things in the hope of feeling connected, understood, and loved by others. Many times, people compete with others as to whose life is more challenging and difficult. This also breeds a sense of connection, but not in ways that manifest a pleasant life. To connect is to become progressively more aware and sacrifice what you need to in order to bring about clarity and love for all things. Although competition is a natural human inner phenomenon, it tends to rule our lives. But from this day forward, we can begin trusting more and fighting less. We owe it to ourselves; we owe it to this planet.

Summary:

Competition is a survival response generated by the inner child. It is intended to make us feel a higher level of self-worth and self-respect. As we feel more successful, we move into more situations to compete, therefore living a life of suffering and rarely ever feeling a sense of inner peace. To compete is to suffer; therefore, to cooperate with all that life has to offer is to bring a new interpretation of love back into our lives. Competing makes us feel like we're achieving more when in reality, we're achieving less of what we truly want, which is cooperation. When we are beyond anxiety, we see farther ahead than what our initial feelings may say. No longer do these initial feelings lead our behaviors since we know where that path leads in the end, and we no longer wish to pay that price. This is true compassion, this is true connection, this is truly living.

Chapter 6 – Finding Your Own God

When I came up with the chapters for this book, I wanted to make sure that I was true to myself and everyone working on living beyond anxiety. Therefore, I needed to separate myself from overthinking each chapter and focus more on what I intuitively felt was best to write about. I simply couldn't leave this newfound relationship with God out of it. Some people may initially become distraught if they perceive me as bringing religion into this book, but I most certainly haven't. You have naturally grown into a relationship with an outer intelligence that none of us can truly understand nor explain, but we sense that it is there. When we are healing, we grow in hope, trust, and understanding. With this inner growth comes an appreciation for the anxiety journey. But appreciation toward whom, or what? That interpretation depends on the individual, and all answers are correct.

God grows more real in a person's life beyond anxiety.

Let me give you an example of how this manifested in my life. For a very long time, I was an atheist, never believing nor being open to the idea that some form of energy could become a part of my life. I thought it was me and only me until I was beyond anxiety, which opened my heart and mind to more possibilities. God began showing up everywhere for me because I was open to communicating. It was in the trees, the wind, the river, the stars, and the clouds. It was everywhere. But not only was God an external presence for me, I realized that we all have a part of God within us since we are the co-creators of our realities.

Beyond anxiety, what we were fed about God changes. Back then, we were slaves to an entity or idea. Nowadays, we work collaboratively with what we perceive to be a helpful life companion. Through our new interpretation of God, we feel protected but not reliant. This is a key transition toward your true self. We feel cared for, and therefore we feel that infinite possibilities are present for us. Take spontaneous remissions, for example, a phenomenon you most likely will not hear much about in the media. Many of the people who've experienced spontaneous healing feel that they were not only given this healing but also worked with an intelligence within them that gave them life. Twofold, a belief in the external along with a belief in the internal that worked harmoniously to bring about a deep emotionally led desire. Did expectation have something to do with their healing? I believe it did as well. Since what we expect tends to be realized much of the time, they expected to heal from their ailments, creating the images in their minds of what they wanted their futures to look like.

When I work with my coaching clients, I never present them with a godly possibility, but they often do. Within a few weeks to a few months of working together, many of them will come to me with a deeper curiosity about their new interpretation of God and the role it may be playing in their healing. When this occurs, my best advice to them is to continue to be open to answers and never allow their old beliefs to divert the path they're on. As we give ourselves permission to explore this newfound world and relationship, we begin to question other core beliefs that are holding us back. No longer do we feel that merging with the beliefs of our parents is a sign of love and loyalty. Rather, the loyalty and love are focused more on what is true for us. Therefore, we can get to a whole new level in our relationship with our parents.

We came to this world as a unique being; let's make sure that we don't leave it as a mold of someone else.

What a shame that would be. Exploration will take you to your true self. I know that as you feel like you are moving beyond anxiety, you are becoming progressively more open to exploring the unfamiliar. During anxiety, anything unfamiliar is rejected; beyond anxiety, what is unfamiliar is respected. This level of respect for what is unfamiliar allows for our perceptions to shift from fear to love. As children, we were such curious beings, but the world became very bland quickly. Our interest in life lessened as we grew older since our bodies felt the need to protect us from making similar "mistakes" to the ones we made in our past. We became chemically protected; our traumas became stored in our subconscious mind and body, and we gradually became overly focused on survival and less interested in creativity and creation.

When you find your own God, you are given permission to become a child again.

Your beautiful and carefree childlike tendencies are then coupled with your adult-minded intelligence to bring about much gratitude for life. If you're beginning to experience this in your own life, all I can tell you is to keep going. Do not block your progress by falling for the interpretations of any friends or family about where you are right now. Do not allow yourself to be a slave to their perceptions and beliefs. You've grown out of this world, and as much as a part of you believes it's safe to go back there, you need to stay open and keep exploring your individuality. Do not go back to a low vibe, but rather embrace the high vibes you are beginning to feel. Living life on your own terms means being accepting of other people's opinions but never allowing them to turn into your own. If one person believes that God can only be represented by an organized religion and you believe the connection can be grown through more spiritual ways, then that is what's true for you, and that is what you must follow.

Summary:

As you can see, this was the shortest chapter, but one of the most necessary in this book. Short, because this path you are currently on will reveal the answers you seek; therefore, there is no need to hear them from me. Necessary because beyond anxiety, our identities and life become an open book, and we must move toward this unfamiliar place every chance we get.

Chapter 7 – An Altered Past

I remember setting a clear and emotional intention toward healing my anxiety disorder one day. It felt like I had planted a seed and unconsciously began watering it daily to meet with the information I needed to supercharge my healing journey. The more I looked for the answers, however, the less clarity I received. So instead, I allowed (key word, *allowed*) the answers to come to me at the time it chose. One morning as I woke up, I had a massive epiphany that I immediately wrote down. I heard a set of words that felt were even louder in my mind than the normal daily pessimistic and catastrophic ideas that had led to constant anxiety. The words were …

"If you had one opportunity to go back and see your past differently, what would you like to see happen instead?"

A little context first before we go deeper. At the time, I was really struggling to find my way. You could say I was barely functional, and I felt like I was on the brink of losing it completely. At the time, I thought the way to heal my anxiety was through willpower and hope that any content I consumed from the outside would somehow trigger something within me to heal. I had never considered the idea that my present could very well be connected to parts of my past.

"Was it possible that my mind and body were simply reflecting on the information it gathered from my childhood years?"

I had always thought that if something was over, it was over. I hadn't consciously kept any real records of my past; however, the part of me interpreting my reality wasn't my conscious mind, at least at the time it wasn't. Epiphany after epiphany started coming over me. Soon, what was a starting point began to grow into other questions such as …

> "What would you like to hear in that moment of trauma instead?"
>
> "How do you wish your father had treated you at that moment instead?"
>
> "What truth do you wish you could have verbalized in that very moment instead of shying away?"

Wow. My interpretation of these epiphanies led me toward even deeper insights. If the mind and body were connected to my past, and my past was a reflection of my perceptions in the present, could I interpret my past differently and therefore shift my present perceptions for good? The answer was a loud and clear yes! I needed to be cautious and aware going forward, however, in the sense that I needed to understand what language the subconscious mind understood in order for change to arise. Logic wasn't going to work. If it did, it would have by that point. Rationalizations from support friends and family weren't going to work either. They had beautiful intentions, and I often relied on their words to get through many days, but deep down, I knew it didn't hold enough emotional weight for change to happen.

If there is no change in the emotional body, there will be no change in the mental, physical, or spiritual body. This was a rule I began living with that spurred on tremendous progress over anxiety daily. Every change I wanted to implant into me needed to be accompanied by emotion since it was emotional suppression that got me to this anxious state, and it was emotional expression that was going to get me out. I began using a chair as one of the few techniques I mastered back then. I used my sense of smell to imagine that sitting across me was someone who somehow negatively affected me from my past, and I began to speak. Not only did I speak, but I also spoke loudly, sometimes shouting. No emotion, no change, I would remind myself. As I spoke to the chair, I told that person how they affected me and what I want our relationship to look like going forward. I forgave them at a heart level (not at a limited mind level). I remember sweating and crying profusely during my chair interactions, which were deep signs of somatic purging. The adrenaline that mobilized my body, which once made me interpret my bodily symptoms as potential illnesses, now began looking harmless. Instead, I welcomed whatever changes my body wanted to make in those moments. I was implementing a form of reframing I use in many of my online programs for healing.

I stopped tippy-toeing around life and felt like a roaring tiger—unstoppable at times. I was respectfully disagreeing with others if that was my truth. I was telling strangers how wonderful their smiles were. I was proving to my inner child that reframing the past and responding intuitively and effectively in the moment was safe and necessary for us both. Many of my clients report a feeling of lightness when they begin down the path of vulnerability. Vulnerability is your friend, I tell them, and they take every chance to embrace that vulnerability with open arms. Some warriors may approach such changes more systematically; others would rather dive right in. I believe this has something to do with the level of suffering and dissatisfaction. People who have hit rock bottom are much more likely to jump right in because they feel they can't afford to carry their heavy emotional baggage around for one more day. Sometimes, I even have to twist the pain button a little to get people to that level of "no return." I ask them what their lives will be like in 20 years if they stay on the anxious path they're on, or how their future relationships will be like if they never forgive the people from their past. This gets them to a state of much deeper rapport with me, and they become much more suggestible, which makes our sessions even more powerful.

Remember, going beyond anxiety means perceiving what you've been hanging onto differently at a subconscious level. Only then can positive healing momentum be on your side.

Of course, it wasn't solely about reframing parts of my past to bring about resolution. Healing is a puzzle that demands every piece to be in place. Only then can we be set free to be who we were meant to be—free. The other parts of my life that needed changing were:

- My ability to tap into optimism about a future event, therefore overriding the pessimism.

- My ability to guide my inner child to see beyond catastrophe and toward neutrality.
- The willingness to verbalize my anger and other emotions productively and respectfully so that I no longer repressed my emotions in my body.
- My ability to stay consistent with my new morning and evening habits so that I could bring my nervous system to a point of peace and balance once again.
- The awareness to think but not overthink, therefore allowing my thinking and intuitive sides to work in harmony.

What was interesting during my initial epiphany, and following through with the reframing process, was that the next steps became easier and easier for me. Even though there appeared to be a long list of pieces that fit into the anxiety-healing puzzle, they didn't feel like an effort to do. Rather, because I enjoyed personal progress so much, I was being led toward each next step for me to find myself again. Many anxiety sufferers become overwhelmed by the entire healing puzzle because anxiety is already mentally, physiologically, and spiritually overwhelming. So much so that they never get started. Rather, I would work with the initial epiphanies that come from planting an emotional intention and see where it takes you next.

If healing isn't enjoyable, you will never heal.

Beyond anxiety, we understand this deeply. We enjoy our healing journey and never want to see ourselves as truly healed, but rather always healing. Prior to going beyond anxiety, I felt that I needed to locate the source or motivation of my automated anxiousness and anxious behaviors. As I planted this seed of intention, a question within me arose once again …

"What is the greater purpose around these anxious feelings and emotions, and how do they serve me?"

Powerful. My conscious mind answered, *It serves me not; enough is enough!* But the subconscious side of me knew very well that anxiety symptoms regularly produced would keep me from attempting things that led me to failures and mistakes in the past. They would keep my belief systems merged with a parental figure I looked up to and kept my life restricted, so to speak. So much unconditional love and protection coming from the inner child's subconscious mind; it truly is mesmerizing as I look back now. I remember feeling saddened by how I treated the feelings that arose within me back then. Those feelings weren't there to do harm, not at all. The worse my relationship got with those feelings, the more my anxiety rose. The more my anxiety rose, the more rapidly my feelings turned into emotions, leaving me helpless to the actions that followed.

When anxiety becomes the default way of experiencing our days, the ability for our conscious mind to thoughtfully redirect our focus and perceptions becomes weakened. This is why it blows my mind when I hear people today consistently refer to anxiety as a mental health problem. Retaining the label that anxiety is a mental health problem turns off the ability for sufferers to tap into their inner resources that will lead to long-lasting change. The mental side of things is just a piece of a larger puzzle, and to tell an anxiously emotional person that changes in their thinking is the only way to manage their anxiety is limiting, to say the least. It helps, sometimes greatly, but oftentimes there is other, deeper work to be done. This work emphasizes calming the mind and body to the point where the subconscious mind becomes progressively more open to suggestion (which is the best time to use affirmations for healing). Altered state work, where we allow our brainwave states to move from high beta (highly engaged and deep thinking) to more theta (calm and open-hearted), allows us to understand where the roots of our anxiety disorder truly lie. I often use my mapping technique (search "Mapping The Anxiety Guy" on YouTube) as a starter for anxiety sufferers to begin building a better relationship with their symptoms and their bodies. This technique will allow your nervous system to calm itself, compassion to once again arise, and the answers to your clear intentions for healing to appear over time.

These are just a few suggestions to begin to go beyond anxiety. When I look for anxiety healing techniques, I have some very important items that need to be checked off for me to take them on:

- It must work fast.
- It must affect the subconscious mind.
- It must have the potential for deep emotions to arise.
- It must come with a degree of discomfort.
- It must have the feeling of being repeatable.

If anyone thinks true healing is a linear and comfortable path, they are mistaken. There will be discomfort, and more challenges will arise at the beginning stages than you thought would. Many people think that they'll begin feeling better right away because they're doing the self-care work. Nothing could be farther than the truth. It's likely that you will be met with disturbing and metaphorically driven dreams from the subconscious mind about what needs to be resolved, as well as heightened anxiety reactions by the inner child in moments that would normally feel neutral or even pleasant and excessive tiredness and spontaneous moments of needing to cry. But in the end, is it all worth it? You better believe it. Winston Churchill said it best:

"If you're going through hell, keep going."

Does it feel like you are going through hell right now while working with your subconscious mind/inner child to bring about changes in perception and belief? Good, keep going. A timeframe for healing does not exist because remember, we are always healing. Right now, you may actually be exactly where you had once hoped and wished you could be, but you're too caught up in how far you still have to go to see your progress. We often dream of greater days to satisfy an inner need to stay in the realm of suffering. This is done out of habit. Of course, there are beneficial habits, and there are not-so-beneficial habits. The addiction to suffering brings many unbeneficial habits, and at its root lies a deep sense of unworthiness for the good. These are not lies so much as they are desires by the inner child to fulfill its goal—to strengthen its interpretation of who we are, what we deserve, and what reality is. These flawed perceptions must be worked with, and we must not allow ourselves to swim in them for long periods of time. Anxiousness, for example, is an emotional state and one we are naturally going to experience from one day to the next. Anxiety, however, is a cycle. It's a constant, a place made of dread that is very much strengthened by the lack of trust we have in the ever-changing realities of life. Beyond anxiety, we are no longer victims of our past but rather beneficiaries of the lessons from them based on our courage to reperceive and resolve. Therefore, our leftover mental and emotional scars that sporadically arise are not signs of setbacks but reminders of how much we've grown. This level of emotional maturity spurs on spiritual growth, which helps us to respect and experience a reminder from the past, but that is as far as it goes.

Beyond anxiety, we are creating our own definitions of love and are no longer limited by the definitions others have given us.

Many people suffering today think that their conscious ideas around love are what is true for them. Little do they realize that love can mean pain, revenge, a desire to be better than, or anything for that matter. These inner child definitions of love are what is fed by a feeling within, not by what we logically think about love. For example, a person gets into a new relationship, and as has been the case in all their other recent relationships, he or she finds ways to sabotage it. There is absolutely nothing wrong with the other person. The connection and rapport are magical, but it could be that they are just too short, or tall, or have a strange tone of voice, or are too demanding (when they may not be at all), too caring, too this, or too that. The sufferer's laser-like focus on the bad fulfills the inner child's definition of love, which falls in line with being argumentative and is based on what they observed of their parent's behavior. In this case, true love centered on unconditional love cannot even be fathomed by the inner child-mind. Not because the inner child doesn't want to take on this new belief, but because the emotional associations to every word in the dictionary have already been embedded deeply within them based on childhood experiences.

The best way to understand your unconscious definitions around a certain term is to ask yourself for an answer to what this term means to your inner child. You could say out loud, or in your mind, *I want to feel what the definition of love means to my inner child*. As you do, notice what feelings arise without trying to intellectually edit them; just observe fully. I remember doing this exercise to understand more deeply what my core beliefs really were, and without fail, I always felt a sense of loss, rejection, and sadness when I looked for the meaning of love. I would even find myself wanting to cry out of sheer sadness. There was always a feeling of unworthiness around the true meaning of love and success in my life. It didn't matter what my adult conscious mind thought because the universe doesn't read logic; it reads feelings and emotions and gives back more daily experiences connected to these. I began finding the roots of my anxiety disorder and why things were never improving in my inner or outer world through this way.

I had begun feeling the answer to that very important question that I asked my inner child/subconscious mind. I was honest with myself and allowed myself to feel it fully (before writing it down), and I intuitively began having a sense of what person or experience from my past it was connected to.

This inner work gets us to begin shifting our emotional associations to words, people, and specific past experiences. When my intuition (heart) was balanced with my intellect (mind) in feeding me answers (and me listening), I began reframing what needed to be reframed. Reframing is the ability to place a new frame around something you've experienced from your past that has something to do with your blocks and worries in the present. I reframed my childhood traumas (read my second book, *F*ck Coping Start Healing*, for the exact technique or go to my YouTube channel's playlist called Reframing Sessions), I did chair therapy, and I did a direct drive exercise that emphasizes the use of one targeted affirmation consistently. The direct drive exercise was powerful in that it got me thinking in line with the words very quickly, but there were a few keys to making this happen for me:

1) Be specific — When you create an affirmation, you can't use sentences like, *My mind is clear, and my body is healing*. These help to some extent, but they aren't personal and targeted enough. Instead, use a more specific affirmation like, *My mind is accepting my new, empowering ideas about myself, and my body is releasing all negative associations toward my father*. The subconscious mind will not accept nor understand generalities; remember that. Focus on what it is you want to change and slightly lengthen your sentences.
2) Think or speak with emotion — A direct drive is just that, a direct intention you want to be manifested from your subconscious forward to your present and future reality. That is why

emotions play such a big part in our convincer strategy. Get emotional, and you will not only be affirming your truth but living it out as well.

3) Keep saying it many minutes after you feel you've done enough — This is key. Repetition shows your deeper side that it must pay more attention to this piece of new information. When you feel you've done enough, do more, then more, and even more. Keep directly affirming what it is that is presently taking place within your change work, and your new identity will be revealed to you.

These three methods I've mentioned are in the category of "primary interventions." Reframing can be done for past events or future events as well (use my powerful YouTube video called "positive energy deep guided meditation" for future reframing purposes). Chair therapy is most effective in its simplest form as we verbalize our truth toward someone while utilizing our imaginative processes to bring them alive within the chair across from us. Direct drives are simple, straightforward, targeted, and repeated affirmations about what is taking place right now in terms of the changes you want to make real at a psychological and physiological level.

An altered past becomes a peaceful present.

Much of our present results are determined by our openness and abilities to reperceive our past, make peace with our parents and other authority figures, and move forward. Going beyond anxiety is like meeting someone new and wanting to get to know that person better. The initial emotional rush will begin subsiding.

What will be left are our abilities to never lose sight of why we are making the changes we are making. Beyond anxiety, we are respectful and appreciative of any intrusive thoughts, bodily anxiety symptoms, or initial survival-led feelings. Beyond anxiety, we nurture these reactions as we would our own children. The truth is that when you can begin treating yourself and the things you dislike about yourself the way you've nurtured and brought up your own kids, you will be free.

Summary:

Altering our past is a big chunk of the inner healing journey. We do it by becoming well acquainted with a few powerful skill sets, and we use the clarity gained from implementing those skills to propel us forward. In the end, it is clarity that heals us, not the skill sets themselves. When we come to a moment when an idea challenges an idea that has not served us well in the past, the question is, what do we do? Most people neglect the newfound clarity and refocus on the ideas that have consistently taken center stage in their lives up to now. However, beyond anxiety, we understand the power behind these moments of clarity and epiphanies, and we understand that they are no accident. They are there as subtle responses by the inner child, letting us know that it sees the efforts you are putting in, and the inner child is slowly getting on board with these new changes. Awareness will set you free from your past. Progressively, we are becoming more aware of what inner work needs to be done and how it is connected to the heavy emotional baggage we've been carrying in our bodies for far too long. Stay aware, stay open to looking directly at what you need to, and inspire yourself and others along the way.

Chapter 8 – Finding Physical Health Through Emotional and Spiritual Health

In today's world, you often have to serve as your own doctor. As you become less reliant on others and more independent on your self-care journey, new insights and experiences will naturally come to you. For example, during anxiety, I thought that physical problems were solely a physical issue. Beyond anxiety, I've recognized that physical issues mirror emotional issues. Not only that, but I've grown into a world I never knew existed, which was having a spiritual body as well. If someone is emotionally healthy, they will be physically healthy, but what you see on the surface often isn't reflective of what is really taking place on the inside. Emotionally healthy people look, feel, and think in ways that make them experience optimal emotional health. They don't portray themselves as optimistic while thinking pessimistically and feeling similarly. This internal incongruence sends a scattered signal out toward source energy, which in turn sends a scattered signal back. You must, without any doubt, know exactly what you want and be very clear about how to achieve it prior to taking on this journey of going beyond anxiety. One common problem is that people prioritize their family and friends, their jobs or businesses, their cars and other things they own, etc., before themselves. They barely have time for themselves because everything else has more meaning to them. They do not see themselves as the priority. Then there are those who think they have plenty of time and put off their healing altogether. They rationalize with themselves why it's not the right time, how they're over-worked, or how they don't have the skills to change their inner world. Welcome to the defense mechanisms of the inner subconscious mind, which creatively finds ways to keep a person comfortably stuck in their lives.

If you do not make time for yourself, do not expect a change in your results.

You already knew that though, I just brought it back to your conscious attention. Let me give you an example of when I went from physically unhealthy to emotionally, spiritually, and physically healthy.

As many anxiety sufferers can confirm, one of the most debilitating, life-sucking, and annoying symptoms of anxiety is dizziness (which many times is coupled with depersonalization). Now, to give you an idea of what the dizziness felt like for me, think about being on a rocking boat with relentless winds and waves that never stop. Now, add the kind of short-term memory loss some people experience from time to time, like where they forgot they put their keys even though they had them a few minutes prior, all the time. Finally, couple these two experiences with losing touch with all your senses. You reach to touch something but can't feel or describe what you're touching; you can hear but can't make out the exact sound; you can see but don't really know how to perceive what it is you see.

Welcome to the world of dizzying anxiety.

This dizziness, so common with anxiety sufferers, is a chemically protective response to one too many traumatic events. And it's important for you to understand that inner and outer overload is perpetuated by more fighting and overthinking. The more you worry about this symptom, the more future scenarios you will find that will be affected by having it. The more you look to end this symptom, the more signals you are giving to your nervous system to keep dizziness around. In essence, it's there as a sign of emotional baggage overload as well as a protective response to doing something that you may regret later on.

The epiphany that came to me one day was fueled by one inspiring word that rang loud and clear through my mind—*guide*!

Guide? At first, I didn't understand how the word guide could help me with this dizzying sensation of anxiety. But after a little more time of trusting and listening, I understood. To eliminate this symptom, I needed to guide it as if it were a lost soul itself. I needed to work with the dizziness rather than against it and understand why it was there from an emotional perspective as well. It truly is amazing what insights we can reveal when we just open up to having them. So the journey began.

- I spoke to my dizziness.
- I guided my dizziness toward a neutral perspective over what it deemed as threatening.
- I allowed it to heal when it felt the time was right to do so.

I didn't force. I didn't berate. I didn't self-victimize because it was there. I did everything in an opposite and creative way, and it worked! I realized something important through this journey of healing my dizziness symptom of anxiety: That I could build a better relationship with my symptoms, release myself from my previous perfectionistic approach to life, and find self-compassion. I no longer saw the symptoms as signs of future ill health, but parts of me that were looking for guidance. This journey of healing my dizziness led me straight toward spirituality, mainly because I felt I was also being taken care of while I was taking care of these parts of myself. The more emotionally and spiritually healthy I became, the more my body responded positively.

How could this be?

We live in a world where emotional expression is frowned upon, mental-health issues are seen as weakness and neediness, and spirituality is seen as kooky. We've become a numb society in many ways, never looking deeper into our own potential and what life could be like out of fear of indifference from others. Fear finds more things to be fearful of; love also finds more things to fall in love with. These are our choices. To become physically healthy as every one of us wishes, we must dare to be different.

The path to inner freedom demands courage, followed by a sense of neutrality.

We don't move from sad to happy or from fear to love; we go from sad to neutral to happy, and from fear to neutral to love. When we feel neutral at a mental and emotional scale, our old, limiting childhood beliefs no longer drag us around. Rather, the playing field is even. At this point, one judgment is no stronger than another, and one option is no stronger than another. This is where the control we seek begins manifesting. We are then starting to choose which reality we want to live in, rather than allowing the world to decide for us. Life begins to have meaning, and our physical health is no longer priority number 1. Certainly, we wish to be optimally physically healthy, but we no longer feel the need to do all the right things all the time to meet this desire. Instead, we trust that because we feel different and better, we are progressing. Our physical bodies are catching up to the new changes because it's the body that is always playing catch up with the mind (conscious and subconscious).

Trust is strengthened, uncertainty is befriended, and anything unfamiliar is respected rather than judged harshly.

Many of us complain that life is too short, when in fact, the way that many of us live reflects being dead already. What difference is there between someone who is already dead and someone living within the comforts of daily discomfort? There is no difference. Yes, they are physically present, but not mentally or otherwise. Until we are honest with ourselves, there will be no change; we will never go beyond anxiety because we will always be using our anxiety as an excuse for not being able to do the things we must. Anxiety can become a "get out of jail free" card. Perhaps it shows up as fewer work hours because of an unfulfilling job, less socializing because others are more "high vibey" than you or more self-victimizing behaviors that fall in line with whichever parent you merged with when you were a child.

Are you using anxiety as a get-out-of-jail card? If so, stop!

My physical health dramatically improved when I put that card away and began facing what I feared. Having slept on the streets because of a fear of poverty, for example, may have been a little extreme, but it proved to me how false my beliefs were. We don't face our fears out of a fear of failing, and as a result, our self-worth is lowered even more. However, the future guilt of not taking these necessary steps will weigh much heavier than anything else that we can use as motivation today.

Can you physically heal without tapping into your spiritual side? Yes, you can. There is no rulebook that says that a spiritual guide is a must for self-development or physical healing. Having said that, however, many people are naturally drawn to spiritual growth as they progress forward. They realize how their minds have blocked this connection for far too long. And when they take the time to become more heartfelt, they begin recognizing the potential that life has to offer. I'm not referring here to a "happy" life; rather, I'm referring to a life where you sort for what could go right, what you're grateful for, and how you can better this planet. These are challenging habits to create when our focus is constantly tuned into our physical health and possible threats in the future.

When we are beyond anxiety, we no longer strive for physical health. What we do for our health is out of pure enjoyment, not for any other purpose than that. However, while suffering from anxiety, our obsessive-compulsive tendencies may very well be activated, causing us to do everything just right and nonstop to meet the goal of feeling optimally healthy, but we never seem to reach this goal. We give ourselves much to do that takes up our attention and time, and yet we rarely experience any enjoyment while doing these things for ourselves. I've learned that a goal fueled by an intention is important; however, becoming obsessed with the goal fuels our need for certainty and control, which eventually works in reverse, causing us to feel physically and emotionally depleted. Once an intention and a goal to have optimal health is set, our mission must be to let go and trust that it will manifest when it wants to. This is done by giving ourselves fully to the moment of whatever we are doing for ourselves. When we give, we receive. When we strive for and check our results constantly, we are disappointed and left with more bewilderment and confusion.

A physically healthy body is an emotionally healthy body; there's no way around it.

It's unfortunate, though, that as Dr. John Sarno mentions in his excellent book, *The Divided Mind* (highly recommended read), only up to 20% of people will ever make the connection between their suppressed emotions and the result that is their physical body. How can they not, though? A doctor's word is law. Look for clarity from a doctor (bless them for the important work they do daily) around your physical ailment, and you'll be met with a high degree of focus on the symptom, the pain, the discomfort, and the ache, but never the root of the ailment.

Take, for instance, my conversation with a woman named Lori, who was an anxiety sufferer. She came to me at the height of her anxiety disorder, looking for guidance and help. She told me all the things she "had" first:

"I have panic disorder, health anxiety, and I also have constant aches and pains in my body every day," she said.

As I was looking to create a "state break" at that moment to halt the negative momentum she was building up, I replied, "No, in fact, you don't 'have' any of these. You were given the label of panic disorder because you are reliving your past emotional traumas in the present moment. You are misinterpreting your anxiety symptoms, which sometimes causes you to 'stand guard' at every bodily reaction you have, and your body aches because of a lack of courage to express what you've been suppressing verbally and emotionally for far too long."

Boy, did that get her attention. The biggest problem we have in the coaching and therapy world today is that the coach or therapist consistently gives the sufferer just what they expect. So I wanted to create some confusion within her immediately to get her to open up to new perceptions. As is naturally the case, her inner child defense mechanisms to change kicked in. Lori said, "Yes, but (key defense mechanism term) it's just all so hard to deal with every day, I just don't know what to do."

These are the words of anxiety sufferers verbalizing not the truth but what they perceive as being the truth based on the stories they and others have fed them about themselves for far too long.

"So why do you do it, then?" I asked. "Why do you do what you do daily that keeps you staying so stuck emotionally and physically?"

After a few minutes of silence and plenty to think about, she replied. "Because I'm afraid of bringing out the real me."

Bingo. I learned that Lori had experienced a series of events early in life that created a core belief within her that said, *Don't be your true artistic, funny, carefree, loving self because others aren't that way, and you have to be like other people to fit in*. She had been wearing a mask for far too long. She had been trying to please everyone but herself and tippy-toeing through her days, hoping not to feel the rise of emotions that left her feeling inadequate and disconnected from others. Every time an opportunity presented itself for Lori to be her true self, she felt a physical itch, ache, or pain, or she noticed a thought tied to the consequences of stepping back into her true self. These were defense mechanisms brought on by her inner-child subconscious mind-body. She had suppressed so many ideas, words, feelings, creativity, expression, and traumas that it all seemed normal to her to be this way.

As we worked together, she began connecting her lack of expressiveness as a whole to her physical complaints, and over the next few weeks, began courageously stepping out of her inner thought-based comfort zones. Lori started talking to her parents about the lack of a family dynamic she wished she had when young and was pleasantly surprised by their understanding. "Better late than never," Lori told me when she shared about the new direction they were headed as a family. She also began taking singing and dancing lessons—something she had always wanted to do but had talked herself out of—and found that people were very accepting of her true self during class. In fact, her classmates showed a high level of willingness to connect with Lisa outside of the lessons as well.

As the days went on, Lori piled up more and more wins in favor of her being true to herself. These wins didn't just mean she had more pleasant life experiences; it meant that her subconscious mind-body, led by the beliefs held by the inner child, was becoming malleable. Those beliefs were changing, but they were changing naturally, not forcefully. She had a sense that a high degree of focus on creating change at that very moment was not necessary. Rather, she did what she had to do and trusted that over time the pieces of the puzzle that led to being her true self would fall into place one by one, and they did.

As Lori made the journey beyond anxiety, she was experiencing revelation after revelation, epiphany after epiphany. As her mental and emotional body improved, so did the state of her physical body. The transformation to a new identity and a whole new inner world is complete when a person owns what they're feeling. Commonly, though, when an anxiety sufferer begins to reap the rewards of their self-care efforts, they have a sense that the new feeling is fleeting and will leave them soon. But the people who are able to make inner peace as natural a state as anxiety once was for them own what they feel without allowing the mind to edit what may or may not arise in the future. Intelligence can perpetuate anxiety. When coupled with primal instincts set on overdrive, it can drive away a person's trust in their intuitiveness. Intuitively, they may know what to do for themselves or others, but due to a lack of trust in the voice of their heart, they revert back to what's familiar.

Lori's biggest realization was that not everything will go her way in life, and that's the beauty of it all. She no longer woke up in the morning clinging to what she had but instead creatively looked to build on what she had. If she felt a sense of inner peace, she welcomed it. If she had some anxiousness, she worked with it. One wasn't any better than the other. Lori transformed her identity one trusting step at a time. She no longer clung to being a "somebody." She was OK being a nobody. Her ego had dissipated to the point where she no longer labeled herself in self-defeating ways. Her body regained the energy it once had, and her aches were no longer as overwhelming as they once were.

You can feel anxious without feeling that you are anxiety.

That's an important distinction and one that has a massive effect on the emotional and physical body. Anxiety sufferers mentally (and therefore emotionally) build on the feelings of anxiousness through catastrophizing, mind reading, and fortune-telling; people who live with inner peace don't. They experience moments of consciously or unconsciously driven anxiousness and have a level of awareness that intuitively brings them toward the proper way to respond to the feeling. When healing is present, we become increasingly more comfortable in our own skin, and we no longer feel the need to hide our emotional scars. We become proud of what we've achieved because it's a massive achievement. I believe the addiction to suffering is right up there with an addiction to today's street drugs; there is a reliance on it out of pure safety, familiarity, and a feeling of certainty. Anxiety is the worst use of our imagination. The truth that many of us have concluded on this journey is that we can, in fact, consciously imagine a better future outcome rather than unconsciously reverting to the worst possible one. This practice brings us toward a new addiction—inner peace and contentment.

Summary:

When we understand that the emotional body is the physical body, a whole new world will open up to us. With this understanding, we no longer deny our emotional states but recognize the consequences of suppressing our emotions and the harm it does to the physical body. From this point on, we are more caring and gentle toward ourselves as we slowly release the emotional bag we've been carrying in our bodies that has caused our minds to work against us. We begin forgiving people from our past and reorganizing how we perceive specific troubling experiences we may have had before. As we diet the emotional body, we feel a sense of lightness coming over us. This is a good thing to bring to your awareness. We find that struggle no longer serves a purpose, and we begin putting things into perspective, such as understanding that our needs were really just wants after all. As the mental, emotional, and physical bodies find harmony with each other, there is a reconnection with our spiritual sides.

When this occurs, it's vital to embrace this new connection and become comfortable with the feeling of walking in the dark for the next little while until discomfort turns into comfort. In the end, what anxiety really is is an energetic imbalance. When these aspects of you come together and work as one, balance is created on the inside. From this moment on, miracles are no longer seen as miracles but regular occurrences based on the type of message you're sending toward the intelligence that lives within you and outside of you in nature.

Chapter 9 – Making Peace with Silence and Darkness

During my anxiety disorder, there was a time when any kind of silence felt wrong, and I just had to have noise around me. At that time, I also remember having an uncomfortable relationship with the dark, so at night, I would open and close my eyes multiple times in case bad entities appeared. The idea of making peace with silence and darkness never occurred to me. I did all I could to cope with the situation and make time go by as fast as possible, which led me once again to the old familiar pain and inner suffering. I was not comfortable with silence because I had emotional associations toward it that kept me on high alert, such as:

- Silence is unproductive, and being unproductive is lazy.
- When things were silent, it was inevitable that something was going to go wrong.
- Silence brings about loneliness and, therefore, depression, so any sort of noise kept me away from this depressive state.

These were stories. Nothing more than stories I repeatedly told myself that I began believing. As humans, we have the potential to believe anything about anything. Were these stories around silence true? Were they a product of my upbringing? Did I create these out of the blue? What was most important wasn't the answers to these questions but what I needed to do to alter them. When it came to creating new associations toward silence, that's exactly what I did.

During my initial years of healing my anxiety, I began running tests to prove to myself whether what I believed was true or not. One of those tests started by first having a neutral and accepting attitude toward both sides of the story—silence is bad, silence is good. I would enter into a state of complete silence to first prove to myself that I could build up a new relationship with this state. Over time, I spent more and more time in silence, never identifying with being a monk or a spiritual guru or anything like that, but to simply see whether my core beliefs held any truth behind them. As you can imagine, they didn't. Beyond anxiety, I realized that silence teaches; it never takes anything worthwhile away. I recognized that the voice of my heart, which was my intuition, my empathic abilities, my psychic abilities, and my ability to manifest what I wanted, all grew stronger thanks to silence. Silence taught me that I could be myself, not the version of myself everyone else wanted to see. That was a revelation, to say the least.

To have either short or long moments of silence within each day helps us to receive the answers we've been longing for through other people.

Beyond anxiety, we are simply building better relationships—better relationships with our own inner child, with our bodies, with our minds, with our spirits. As we better our internal relationships, our external relationships improve as a result because our brain's filter system is now working out of love and understanding rather than threat and competition.

During anxiety, anything and anyone has the potential of letting us down, being better than us, or making a fool of us. Beyond anxiety, anything and anyone has the potential of teaching us, healing us, and connecting us to greater wisdom within.

Making peace with silence doesn't happen overnight, but it must happen nonetheless. The person no longer finds ways to distract from the very thing they've been running from all this time, which is themselves. Rather, through silence, they become gentler with their words and actions toward themselves, and, in turn, all possibilities for a bright future are present. When practicing building a new and accepting relationship with silence, there are a few steps you must take:

1) Find a place where you won't be distracted by other people and loud noises.
2) Turn your attention toward one thing. This could be the rhythm of your breath, your posture, a safety color you'd like to inhale throughout your body, or even a word that you turn into a repeated mantra.
3) Practice letting go and stay focused on your one thing. When your attention wavers, bring it back to your one thing.
4) Start with 1 minute daily and gradually build up daily, weekly, or monthly from there.

You will learn at least one valuable lesson from each silent session you have. This lesson may strike you right away or days later. Either way, it's important that you write down all of these lessons to cement the intention you've made to heal and find deeper meaning. Silence is the gateway to courage, and courage is the ingredient that leads to an open heart. When your heart is open to all perceptual possibilities, you no longer fall for irrational fear; you no longer are led toward anxiety. The beauty of this path is that the time you spend thinking or imagining the worst possible conclusions will lessen dramatically. Weeks spent in fear turn to days, days turn to hours, hours turn to minutes, and minutes turn to seconds.

This is all possible simply by building a more loving and understanding relationship with silence.

Many of you will be able to understand that this is a natural byproduct of targeted self-care. This book is highly focused on what to expect while healing and going beyond living with anxiety, so you can expect to progressively become more comfortable and loving toward yourself as time goes on. Also, remember that these are skill sets that often naturally form through prioritizing your overall health. Beyond anxiety, you will often surprise yourself. Mentally, you will surprise yourself in how you begin thinking about things. Emotionally, you will surprise yourself by how you begin experiencing a loving emotional state instead of a cautious and fearful one. Imaginatively and spiritually, surprises will also arise. Don't let the discomfort of these surprises bring you back into a familiar and painful past. Rather, keep exploring them with the curiosity of a young child before the child was corrupted by the belief systems of others.

Introducing Uncle Seref.

I have an uncle. Well, we call him Uncle, but he's really a long-time family friend named Seref. At the time of writing this book, Seref is 82 years old with an energy level that would make a typical 35-year-old jealous. Being a natural observer of human behavior, I became increasingly aware of the habits that led to such a vibrant lifestyle that Uncle Seref was living. But I wanted to find out the truth, the secret for such a zest for life, so I asked him one important question.

What is the secret to staying forever young?

His answer was threefold:

1) "Replace fear with curiosity."
2) "Find purpose, and don't wait for it to find you."
3) "Be true to yourself no matter what."

I also found out that Uncle Seref takes time every day to connect with silence, which was a big surprise to me. At the time, I was surprised because he was very socially active and so full of zest. Back when I was suffering from anxiety, I thought people who meditated or connected with silence were antisocial and highly introverted. It wasn't the case at all. This was another massive lesson for me to give up the labels that held me hostage to my old belief systems. If I was going to heal, I realized that sacrifices needed to be made, and none were bigger than what I believed about who I was, what I deserved, and what reality was.

The point I'm trying to drive home through this chapter is that silence can be your friend. The better friends you become with silence, the greater the insight you will gain. When this insight begins snowballing your way, you stop looking for answers from others and trust that you already know.

The mind thinks it knows, while the heart truly knows.

When I thought about darkness, I was faced with another challenge. My heart sense would consistently remind me that this was another roadblock that I needed to make peace with to continue on my path toward going from maintaining my "somebody" reputation to becoming nobody, followed by being connected to everybody. Naturally, when a person is beyond anxiety, many aspects of their lives fall in line with the positive changes that are being made; this includes a new perception about darkness. During my anxiety days, the dark was evil because my subconscious or inner child connected it to the characters in many of the horror flicks we know well, such as Jason in *Friday the 13th* and Freddy Krueger in *A Nightmare on Elm Street*.

As a child, I wondered how I ran into these movies and why these villains always showed up at night.

Your negative associations to darkness could have come from somewhere else. No matter the case, making peace with the dark is necessary for continued inner growth. Beyond anxiety, there is a willingness to step into the unfamiliar future rather than run back to a familiar past (suffering). I remember sitting in the dark in my bedroom with a calm presence, asking the worst to happen if it may. To my surprise, nothing happened. Disinterest arose around fear, and when we can become disinterested in what we once feared, we are home free to build on any new belief we choose. So I sat, and sat, and sat. I remember purchasing the darkest facemask available just to practice making peace with the dark, and it worked brilliantly. As much as my mind wanted to get me out of the situation, I assured it that change was safe, this moment was safe, and my emotional state backed up my actions, which was crucial for me to go beyond anxiety. We often expose ourselves to something, but we forget that it's the feeling we get from the experience that either keeps the fearful belief alive or gets replaced with a more neutral and positive meaning.

When you expose yourself to your fears, make sure you are fully open to both interpretations—fear and safety in that moment.

This openhearted approach will lead to an open-minded one. The inner chatter will subside over time once the mind reads that your feelings toward the fear are more neutral, more grounded. Beyond anxiety, we no longer distract from the darkness or silence by reverting back to our mobile phones. In today's hectic world, you'll frequently notice that a person will be on their phone until the very last few seconds prior to sleep. This is due to fear and nothing more. They are afraid of being present, with the dark, with themselves. They don't enjoy the last few moments before sleep but instead, cling to whatever can stimulate them the most (social media), and then they wonder why their quality of sleep is never ideal. These people wake up exhausted no matter how long they sleep because they are always running from their fears. In fact, it's easier to face your fears daily than it is to run, and your nervous system will thank you for having to do less work.

"Those who fear the darkness have no idea what the light can do." — Katasai Rakshasa

The truth is, warrior, we are just as afraid of our full potential as we are of our imagined irrational fears. Many of us don't know how others will react to us should we thrive effortlessly through life rather than struggle and fight for everything. A good example of this in my own life was during my early 20's when I was looking to become a professional tennis player. Every time I played flawlessly, I would apologize to my opponent. Every great shot was followed by an "I'm sorry" because I simply wasn't familiar with this high level of tennis. I constantly brought my level back down to others because the thought of feeling disconnected from them caused me great fear. This is what separates the very small percentage of people in this world who are truly happy with their lives compared to the vast majority who are stuck in an addiction to suffering. The happy ones don't care what others think, and therefore others become drawn to their courage. The unhappy ones are looking to match the collective low vibration that is within many of the communities today in the hope of gaining what they were never able to gain when they were kids—a sense of acceptance, belonging, and connectedness.

People will find positive or negative ways to fulfill their human needs. The problem is that it's easier to meet needs through negative ways than it is through positive ones.

Summary:

Beyond anxiety, silence and darkness are our friends. You may or may not have had a rocky relationship with either, but it is worth noting in this book how new relationships and, therefore, meanings can be built with both. You don't have to be a committed monk to sit in silence within darkness. All you need are brief moments of courage and curiosity around what seems unfamiliar and unknown to you. Isn't that the greatest change of all when we are beyond anxiety? Our abilities to naturally and effortlessly override our instinctual fear response and turn it into just another life experience. Time does not heal what needs healing, nor does it change the negative associations we've built on from our childhood upbringing. We heal what needs to be healed alongside an external intelligence that reads our deepest intentions through the feelings and emotions we give off from moment to moment. Wake up each morning with the intention to tap into your inner resources that will bring about certainty on this healing path, not confidence. Confidence wavers; it comes and goes. To be certain around the new behaviors and habits you are building means that you cannot fail anymore; there is no such thing. Within every setback, you will find the win, and within every win, you will learn something new about yourself, so just keep going.

Chapter 10 – Beyond the Physical

When discussing the energetic connection to life itself, some people have differing opinions based on their own life experiences. Because this is the case, I'm going to do my best to share with you what I and many others who have healed anxiety have come in contact with regarding energy.

What is energy in relation to being human?

The human energy field is a highly organized information processing system that contains information encoded within it. It carries specific codes that get interpreted by your own nervous system along with other people's nervous systems you come in contact with. Everything we do energetically is a parallel to what we do physically. Everything that exists within this world is a form of energy, and the only difference is its vibration (speed and frequency). Wherever the mind, our feelings, and emotions go is where energy flows. The body does not generate the energy field, but rather the energy field generates the body. Most of the time, it is repressed emotion and recurring thoughts that clog up our energy. These are things you haven't accepted, reframed from the past, or let go of yet. The beauty of unclogging a person's energy and bringing optimal health back to the body begins and ends with personalized interventions that lead to crying, spontaneous laughter, sweating, and sometimes even coughing. True spiritual and, therefore, personal growth and development means moving toward the stuff that causes you pain, the information your instincts are telling you to avoid looking at and moving toward. There are two things each of us can do with energy, give it and receive it. Our breathing rhythms mirror our energetic rhythms, which places a tremendous amount of importance on how we breathe to bring about inner harmony. Tight muscles are a product of shallow and fight or flight related breathing, which leads to energy stagnation. When energy stagnation is present, it can feel like you have one foot on the gas pedal and one foot on the brake simultaneously. This can lead to overwhelm and extreme tiredness even after a full night's rest.

If you are paying attention to something, you are, in turn, sending energy to it. This is an intention read by your subconscious mind.

This is a big reason why anxiety sufferers often cannot escape anxiety. They are always focused on and checking in with their anxiety identity to ask permission to do something new. I tell many of my clients going through my programs, "If you surround yourself solely with quotes, videos, podcasts, conversations, etc., focused on anxiety, you will never heal your anxiety." It is important to note this because freedom is going beyond anxiety toward knowledge and feedback that leads to an upgraded you—your true divine self. In this chapter, we will tap into what it's like to go beyond the physical during the process of overcoming anxiety.

First, let's look at one of my favorite imagery-based exercises for eliminating negative energy. You can start using this today. I call it the negative energy cleanser. Here are the steps:

1) Close your eyes.
2) Relax your eyelids, relax your body.
3) Imagine negative energy coming in from the outside in any way that feels real to you.
4) Imagine using daggers and swords to cut each piece of negative energy coming into your body.
5) When all the energy has been cut off, you are free to imagine that you are walking away and into the most calming and safe environment you know.
6) Stay in this place for as long as you'd like, engaging in all that surrounds you.
7) Open your eyes and stay in this state throughout the rest of your day.

Imagery exercises give us the opportunity to bypass the security guard within our brains called the critical factor. This security guard looks to strengthen and keep alive our limiting beliefs we picked up during childhood. The more relaxed a person is, the more engaged they can be in these types of imagery exercises. It's also important to note that when you use your body in conjunction with your imagery exercises, it becomes that much more powerful and convincing to your subconscious mind (acting out what you are imagining that is happening).

Since so much stagnant energy gets stuck in the head, combing can be a very effective and enjoyable practice that can be used each morning upon waking up to move the flow of energy throughout your body. All you have to do is take both of your hands and touch the ends of your middle fingers with each other, and pretend that you are combing your energy field all the way from the top of your head down to the tips of your toes. Just 2 minutes of combing will give you a sense of inner balance and release much of the stuck energy in your head. For proper energy hygiene, I also wash my hands with saltwater prior to and after combing (search "5 minute energy release The Anxiety Guy" on YouTube for the guided version of this exercise).

An important point to make when a person is transitioning away from a negative energy field and toward a more positive one is that until you have significant emotional experiences that convince your inner child of safety instead of fear, you will constantly sort for what is familiar. What's familiar for an anxiety sufferer is picking out what worst outcome could arise through an inner thought or bodily symptom or any external situation. This is why thought alone cannot alter a set fear-based identity; there's simply not enough juice behind the thought alone to convince the subconscious to believe something different. Thoughts, feelings, words, behavior, or imagination coupled with emotion lead to the master key that makes healing feeling natural rather than forced.

As a former anxiety sufferer transitions toward inner peace, they begin understanding these energetic nonphysical laws better:

1) Law of vibration — Everything has a frequency to it that attracts what is in harmony with it.
2) Law of relativity — Perspective is everything. It's not what happens to us or around us; it's

how we choose to perceive it that leads to the energy we give off and receive.

3) Law of cause and effect — Everything has a beginning, a cause, a root that eventually grows into an effect, a result. Anxiety didn't form out of nothing, and going beyond anxiety didn't happen by accident.
4) Law of polarity — Everything has opposing sides to it. Black has white, good has bad, and anxiety has inner and outer peace.
5) Law of gestation — Everything takes time to develop like a baby in the womb. If you are now beyond anxiety, you can look back and recognize how the new you took time, patience, and relentlessness to develop. Be proud of yourself.
6) Law of rhythm — To manifest what we want, we must be in rhythm or harmony with it. We cannot desire change and yet fear change at the same time. We must be understanding and accepting of all that comes with change in order to have it.
7) Law of transmutation — Everything goes through certain changes before it becomes its final form. When connecting this law to anxiety, we can see how depression, loneliness, and other states of being come to be during the transition to becoming more than anxiety in the end.

These are the laws that govern the universe. Beyond anxiety, we understand and apply these laws many times without conscious awareness, which is fine. However, it is sometimes necessary to focus in on one specific law and implement what we need to do to be in harmony with its teaching.

Beyond anxiety and beyond the physical.

When the vast majority of people overcome anxiety, they begin seeing the world much differently than they used to. During attachment and struggle, everything is an object, a thing. Beyond anxiety and suffering, there is heightened awareness of the energy being given off of everything. The interesting thing when it comes to the negative energy vibrating off of a human being is that we have two choices on how to respond:

1) We can distance ourselves and run from it.
2) We can look to override it through our presence and our commitment to who we are becoming.

The ones who look to run from negative energy are still living in a world of prevention, looking to prevent bad things from happening to them. When a feeling of certainty around our new identity arises, and we sense that the energy we are giving off cannot be negatively manipulated by anything or anyone, we no longer run or distract from negative energy. At this beautiful point, we are grounded within the teachings of nature. It's never the person, thing, or situation that causes us to live with anxiety; it is always our emotional associations to the external. If we associate a person with a low vibration as a threat to our high vibration, we live a life of fear. However, if we associate a person with a low vibration as someone who is lacking the information, guidance, or presence of someone with a high vibration, we, in turn, become that person who can at least show them the way. The rest is always up to them. We can show a person the path to a better life experience, but they are always the ones who must walk that path.

Beyond anxiety, we see the opportunity in everything. During anxiety, we see the lack in everything. Opportunity is everywhere all the time, but you won't see it if your default emotional state is set to fear. Some people may think that they don't have fear. Instead, they think they have anger, depression, or other limiting states. The truth is that they are all a byproduct of a life of fear.

- Anger toward another is anger toward ourselves. We may be disappointed that someone let us down in the past or didn't live up to our expectations in some way. The truth, however, is that you were and possibly are simply afraid of losing something: your reputation, your moment of peace, your finances, your relationships, something. You became angry out of expectation. But what if you had no expectations at all? What if everything that happened or will happen is simply the evidence that you are living? Now, all of a sudden, you no longer have to maintain anything. Instead, your trust and compassion toward the world no longer allow anger to arise or, if it does, it quickly and intuitively gets replaced with neutrality and understanding.
- Depression is also connected to expectation, which is connected to fear. We become depressed as a response to not fully living our life, not having the connections we desire, not fulfilling the life goals set by our parents, or

> otherwise. The key word here is *not*. We are simply not fulfilled. With depression, our life purpose seems to move farther away from us. But what if you were content and formed your own set of beliefs about yourself and life? The depression would begin to lift because you would be opening up your awareness to what you already have rather than focusing on what you've lost or lack. However, the biggest problem with depression is we try to break free from this uncomfortable state immediately and then are consistently disappointed. Rather, what if we gradually and self-lovingly looked to take the next step our intuitive side is encouraging us to take, without any judgment about how we are doing or how far we've come? Soon enough, we would be met with that magical word, momentum, like a train that starts slowly but gains speed over time. You can be that train.

There are two main states a person can live in, fear or love. Everything else is a byproduct of each. Beyond anxiety, we realize how much time and energy we have wasted living in fear, and the clarity gained keeps a person from ever allowing themselves to get caught up in that again. Desire will always be the essential ingredient that leads to releasing the negative energy within and replacing it with love over time. However, desire alone cannot alter a person's energy input and output from fear to love.

Many people desire healing, but the voice of their inner child (subconscious mind) has been so highly respected and followed over time that anything that goes against this voice and its beliefs is met with blocks. This is why you hear so many anxiety sufferers today refer to healing anxiety as being hard. The truth is, it is challenging, not hard. Some people are just too afraid of taking too big of a leap into change, so they convince themselves that it's better to stay where they are rather than take the risk and potentially lose everything. Human beings would rather look to not lose something rather than gain something else. Because this is the case, the only person who can convince an anxiety sufferer that healing is possible and available at any moment is themselves. Your reasons are more powerful than anyone else's, and if you're reading this book right now, having gone through some kind of recent setback that has led to questioning your own healing potential, it's not a setback. In fact, you should delete the word setback from your vocabulary for good. It's the journey, and we're all faced with a handful of very challenging life experiences in this lifetime. For us, we drew the card of anxiety, thankfully, I might add.

Through the inspiring work of the HeartMath Institute, we now understand and can scientifically prove that the human heart is the most powerful generator of electromagnetic energy in the body. The heart is a processor, just like the brain and gut are; therefore, these three processors are potentially the parts of the body that hold onto the most repressed emotions caused by emotional trauma from our past. I've consistently noticed that when people go through the reframing sections of my inner circle program, they tell me that they feel lighter in their mind, stomach, or chest area like a weight has been lifted from these areas. This is a beautiful thing to witness and has a lasting effect on the forming of new core beliefs connected to a person's new identity.

The behavioral result of such deep reframing of past trauma work shows up in a person's life as a more carefree attitude. Going into a café and waiting in line was once an excruciating process for an anxiety sufferer who defaulted to overthinking every aspect of the situation. Healing the past then gives us permission to go back to a time when we were free of self-judgment and a sense of inner heaviness. In that way, the café experience becomes an opportunity to potentially meet someone new, try a new drink, or just covertly share our good vibes with others in line.

The energetic blockages in the body based on past trauma are due to the person at the time being unable to fight back, speak up, or run from and escape the situation. Instead, what happened was the person froze, hyperarousal kicked in, constriction took over the body, and total dissociation arose within the ability to release the energy. This energy then got stored in the body-mind of the subconscious system, ready to remind them of this lesson and look to prevent the same experience from ever happening again.

A person's energy is directly connected to how much trauma is still stored in the body-mind of the individual.

A conscious perceptual shift without signs of emotional release will do very little in helping the inner child re-perceive the situation and life itself. We can be as logical and positive about a situation as we like, but the true key to healing is within altered-state work. Beyond anxiety, we spend more time alone, and we enjoy our own company. During anxiety, the thought of being alone with ourselves for a moment frightens us because we have such a low level of self-worth and are frightened about what may come up. It's true that when you spend more time with yourself and within an altered and calmer state of being, you will potentially be met with things that haven't been resolved yet. It may arise as a thought, a feeling connected to a previous experience, or even a feeling connected to an upcoming experience. All of these come from the inner child, which looks to protect itself from these experiences mimicking past traumas. While doing altered state work, it is presented in the form of a question. The question that the subconscious mind has for the conscious mind is:

Are we ready to finally get over this once and for all?

If the person does what they've always done, the answer would be no, and the past trauma maintains its encoding within the mind and body moving forward. The only way for the answer to be yes is out of awareness and recognition that challenges are opportunities. Unless we see them this way, we can never heal; we will always revert to running from ourselves. When the encoding connected to trauma is altered, when a person has emotionally and therefore successfully been able to alter their perception of the trauma at a subconscious level, only then can the energy field shift. Homeostasis kicks in on the inside, and life experiences begin changing on the outside.

It's amazing how quickly this process can potentially happen. The volcano that's been looking to erupt within finally does as courage defies fear. Beyond anxiety, we no longer *try* things or hope it gets better. We know better than that since these are two of the same things—fear of change being motivated by the inner child. We quickly understand that we have two main parts to us: one stuck in the past that is negatively manipulating the future out of protection and unconditional love, and the other part of us that is intelligent minded, logical, rational, and willfully looks to take on each day being who they crave being but are never truly able to. The inner child vs. the adult mind. This is the inner civil war that contaminates the energetic message being sent out into the universe as to what we want our life to be like.

Place clean water into a cup of dirty water, and you will still get dirty water.

This is why people have an intuitive sense that life should be much more fulfilling and less of a struggle but seem to always be held back by something inside. They begin blaming their boss, their spouse, their circumstances, etc., when, in fact, those are the results, not the causes. The external is never the cause of a person's anxiety or depression; it's always a symptom. The real cause is the two separate internal belief systems taking place fighting for supremacy. However, be warned: The adult mind will rarely, if ever, be able to win a battle of perceptions over the inner child/subconscious mind since one is a new idea compared to another that has been around for decades.

The two components to begin shifting a person's energy come down to reframing and responding. Reframing is our ability to utilize our imaginative processes consciously rather than succumb to the catastrophic imagery we've been acting out unconsciously. As we slow down, as we breathe more deeply, as we relax the body, as we focus on one thing at a time, we slow down our brainwave patterns enough to communicate with the inner child/subconscious mind. At this level of relaxation, we begin to let go of who we are and where we need to be in the future. We are simply curious, holding the intention of going deeper into this stored information and fully present in looking to alter our past or future.

Reframing can be done to set up a more pleasant future experience as well. In my second book, *F*ck Coping Start Healing*, I provided you with a direct link to an emotional reframing practice. In this book, however, I want you to record the script below with your own voice through a microphone of your choice. This way, when you go through the process, it will be that much more powerful. Before we go there, however, we must understand the key elements to a good reframing experience:

1) Basic regression — To bring ourselves *safely* (key word) back to a past experience that needs to be resolved.
2) Vent the emotional charge (related to the event) — This is when we discharge the emotion/energy that has been stored in the body and building for quite some time.
3) Desensitize the event — We no longer feel fear, anger, guilt, blame, etc., when thinking of the past event.
4) Give and receive forgiveness from yourself and others — Whatever happened, there is now forgiveness happening that is directed at you

and others who were a part of that particular experience.

5) Reprocess the experience — Change how you perceive the event completely, and have your feelings align with thought toward this new perception.

These energetic shifts are directly connected to your emotional shifts. The shifts in your emotional state affect your mental state, and these components affect the state of your body. A healthy body is the result of focused attention on these different but connected areas of each person. You can exercise and eat broccoli and greens all you want, but true physical health can only arise when the energetic body is cleansed and the emotional body is in a pleasant state.

Here is the reframing script I would like you to record with your own voice. Make sure you give each step ample time before saying the next one. It's better to lengthen this script rather than rushing to get it done. Don't rush. You need to provide enough time between instructions:

1. Take 3 deep breaths as you relax your eyelids more and more. Your eyelids are becoming so relaxed that it feels natural to just let go of all the tension within them.
2. Now, move that relaxation through your whole body, letting go of all the tension in the body.
3. As you relax the body, you can begin relaxing the mind as you see your thoughts as clouds that come and go. Another cloud of thought appears and disappears over the horizon. And another thought appears and again disappears over the

horizon. It's becoming easier and easier to no longer pay any attention to thought but to being completely absorbed in today's reframing practice.

4. Now, point to where the problem is in the body. Where are you storing these negative emotions connected to fear?
5. What is the color, weight, temperature, size, and texture?
6. How old were you when you first experienced this fear? Go with your first impression no matter what comes up.
7. Are you inside or outside?
8. Is it light or dark?
9. Is there anyone around you?
10. What's happening as you observe it from your adult perspective, looking in on the experience?
11. Walk directly to the younger version of yourself and give them the biggest hug he/she has ever received. Rub his/her back, and notice how much the child needed that hug. Let any emotions that want to arise come up and out now!
12. Look into the child's eyes and tell them the truth about who they are, what they deserve, and what they have to look forward to.
13. Transfer into the child, be the child in mind, body, and spirit in 5, 4, 3, 2, 1.
14. That child needed to say something to someone or do something that he/she didn't get to do at the time because they felt frozen and helpless. If that child could say or do what he/she needs to, what would they do to change the frame of that

experience? DO THAT NOW and TAKE AS MUCH TIME AS YOU NEED.

15. What else does the child need from the adult, or need to do, in general, to feel safer?
16. Is there anything else that needs to be done?
17. Now, take a picture of that moment of safety so that any time you look back and remember this experience, you remember it in a way that makes you feel safe.
18. Take your safety color and spread it over the frame of that picture now.
19. Take 10 breaths and breathe in that safety color and that picture to the part of your body that used to hold onto fear now; breathe out the old color with every exhale.
20. There's a certain sound that you associate with healing. I want you to hear that sound slowly arise within you now, acknowledging that this experience has been transformed and altered for good and for the better.
21. When I count to 5, your eyes will open, lightness will come over you, and any emotions that need purging will be released, like a snake shedding its skin, like old programming being replaced with new programming. Don't question it; just allow your body to do whatever it needs to do to release all of this now.
22. 1, 2, 3, 4, 5, open your eyes.
23. Take a few moments to just be before going about your day.
24. Be gentle toward yourself, and with this gentleness, bring to mind the biggest lesson you just learned about yourself.
25. Well done.

The common theme after reframing done this way is that the person reports they feel lighter. These are the magic words I need to hear to know that the person is soon to be met with further lessons and epiphanies that will only lead to a shift in energy from fear to love.

Soon you will feel attached to nothing and connected to everything.

How many times do you need to go through reframing? The answer is that it must be done for as long as it needs to be done. There is no set amount of repetitions. When a past experience has been dealt with at a feeling level, you may move onto another experience and repeat the exercise with that experience for as long as it takes. Of course, cleaning up the past to live within a creative future and not a set one demands present-moment work as well. This means that as you go about your day, you must attach all fear-based reactions to the ever-loving inner child side of you.

Make sure that you:

- Verbally or internally speak to your inner child during times of driving, letting them see and feel all the miracles within that drive.
- Eat with the inner child, letting them see how wonderful the taste and aroma of the food are.
- Remind them of how any upcoming future event can be seen through the eyes of safety rather than threat.
- Let the inner child know that it's OK to have fun. Spend time by yourself with your inner child building a new loving relationship together.

What I'm asking you do to is bring your inner child with you and communicate safety to them as you go about each day until you no longer have to be so conscious about the process, and it becomes your new default way of living.

The universe has a funny way of revealing its secrets to those people who have the courage to follow their hearts and not their minds. We live in a world where we are forced to look and feel intelligent, but intelligence will overshadow a much greater power that is lying stagnant within anxiety sufferers today, and that is intuition. When intuition, intelligence, and instinct begin working in harmony (with intuition taking up the majority of decision-making and what guides behavior), we have balance. Anxiety is an energetic imbalance; that's truly what it is. The people who have gone beyond anxiety understand this at a deep level, which they couldn't see while suffering because all their time and energy were focused on survival.

You have done a fantastic job at survival, and now it's time to move on, to take a chance on yourself, and go beyond the grips of anxiety toward uncertainty. Within uncertainty is where we learn the most about ourselves and the true essence of life itself. Within certainty, we live in survival, limited, led by all the programming coming from the outside that often doesn't have our best interest at heart. This is a form of slavery. Certainty is slavery; uncertainty is freedom if you can allow it to teach you.

Beyond anxiety, you can expect to fit in less.

Many people see this as a bad thing, but, in fact, you are actually a big part of the creation of a new world and a new direction for mankind. Remember, like attracts like. Your new energy field is always being unconsciously read and examined by everyone else without them even knowing it. As our trust grows in the path that we are on, we become more willing to sacrifice small talk for deeper connections and blame for understanding. Beyond anxiety, no one sees what you see. The confusion on people's faces when you talk about your new energetic connection to nature and life itself will at first confuse you, but quickly that confusion will turn into compassion. Knowing you've opened a door for others to potentially walk through in their future should give you the highest level of self-love. Your presence itself is a message when you are beyond anxiety. This doesn't mean you are always smiling and have no problems. It means you survived and are now thriving in your own unique way. Be proud of yourself and your newfound gentleness toward all that is within life, and there will be no need to go backward again in your life.

Summary:

In this chapter, you were introduced to an imagery-based exercise, a reframing script, and responding work directed at your own inner child. Begin using the negative energy cleanser immediately each day for just a few moments after you wake up, and make sure you take your time going through the process. Also, put the emotional script into your own words and create an MP3 version for yourself to use as often as needed. For many people, this action will be met with a certain amount of doubt. Thoughts such as *It won't be as powerful if I guide myself*, or *I just don't have enough experience with this*, hold no truth within them. Remember, your inner child is very opportunistic, ready to pull you back into a world where you follow what already brings with it a sense of certainty. Do this for yourself, for your future, for the betterment of this world, and lead your inner child toward the truth, which is that you are an infinite being with unlimited capabilities, and this is peanuts. Finally, as mentioned in this chapter, begin at once to create a new relationship with your younger self. Guide them, speak to them (internally or verbally) as you take on the day so that, in time, safety becomes the new default way of perceiving life. You must unlearn what you have been programmed to believe from conception forward. That old software no longer serves you if you want to live in a world where anything is possible. Continue to nurture your soul with each day that passes, as this will create an immediate energetic parallel. Allow like-minded people to come into your life as fast or as slow as it may, as this is a natural effect of the seed of love that you have planted deep within you, warrior.

Chapter 11 – From a Focus on Results to a Focus on Process

In this chapter, my friends, I want to dive into a remarkably interesting phenomenon. I'm talking about turning our focus from gaining results to the actual process that leads to a result. Have you ever noticed how today's digital social media giants such as Facebook and Instagram pit us against each other, which drives the need to come up with better and better posts to gain acknowledgment from their platforms? In a very stealthy way, these platforms create division within society as we no longer feel connected to one another, but rather we become obsessed with a few and pay little attention to the "lessers" within our news feeds. The next dopamine surge is right around the corner as the reward center of our brain recognizes the importance of doing better than the latest post; therefore, we even begin making up stories in the hope of gaining what we never had as a child, acknowledgment. When you live in a results-focused world, you live in a world of suffering. It's never good enough. Everything needs to be bigger, better, healthier, etc., and there is never a moment of being content to see how far we've already come.

Beyond anxiety, there is an unwavering trust that any worthwhile outcome will be met if, in fact, it is worthwhile.

The material world begins fading away as an energetic, more connected world takes its place. No longer is there a fight for answers, but instead a feeling of being guided to them at the moment it's meant to show up. Let me give you a good example of how this took place in my life and its connection to my anxiety at the time.

Roughly 12 years ago, I wanted to eliminate my painful attachment toward my symptoms of anxiety. Each and every waking moment of my life was spent keeping track of my anxiety symptoms and trying to negotiate a deal with them, hoping that my health anxiety would dissipate for good. Within every moment of every day, I was focused on one result—to heal myself. So I searched Google and bought anything connected to a health anxiety success story. I looked for the latest and greatest herb that would help with my deeply self-sabotaging and sensitized state. I even went to such lengths as hiring a personal chiropractor, physiotherapist, and a shaman to lead me toward healing my health anxiety. The one thing I never recognized at the time was that all of these methods have the potential to work for the person who believes that they will. However, at the time, I wasn't in the business of believing. I was in the business of hoping those healing modalities world work out of instinct and survival-based thinking. It was kind of like waiting for a bus at the bus stop and having one after another come and go without ever getting on board. I was hoping for a shift in feeling, but I wasn't willing to look beyond instinct as to what my mindset was toward the methods I was using. In order to get on the bus, you must take a chance on yourself and life. In order for a change to occur, you must look at what doesn't work and commit to the opposite of those ways; therein lies the challenge.

During anxiety, my focus was on "get me the result now," but beyond anxiety, no matter what I was looking to achieve, my attitude was "let's focus on the process toward achieving a result." One of the greatest contributors to this shift for me, and the thousands of others who have healed their anxiety disorder through programs, was slowing down the pace of life. When we slow down, we can see beyond instinct, and intuitive heartfelt messages have the opportunity to contribute to the conversation taking place in the mind. The biggest problem I see with anxiety sufferers today looking to physically slow down isn't so much the inability for them to do so, but rather the emotional associations they hold onto that represent what slowing down means to them. These are childhood core beliefs that look to be fulfilled during each waking moment of the day. Some of these false associations toward slowing down could be:

- If I slow down, I'll never be able to catch up (this belief goes back to the programming in our destructive school systems today).
- If I slow down, people will think I am lazy and unproductive (key word, *people*). Many anxiety sufferers stay anxious due to their fear of not living up to the expectations of others.
- If I slow down, I'll never be successful (as you alter the meaning of success and create your own meaning, you will begin living more in the present and less in a future decided by your past).

Please don't get me wrong. I'm not asking you to physically move at a snail's pace and have no goals or desires in life. My intention is that you look at your life right now and get brutally honest with yourself. Many people have never been deeply honest with themselves ever; they tell themselves one lie after another and believe in them as their life goes on. The healing journey creates separation. This is the most phenomenal thing I've witnessed. There is a natural inclination to separate from how we used to do things and connect with a new way of doing things.

I remember a time when the voice of my heart told me to quit a job I had been in for 10 years even though I had very little in the way of savings and a family that relied on me at a time when positive healing momentum over anxiety was on my side. I listened to that voice and was met with tremendous uncertainty, which led to opportunities I would have never been able to have if I had mentally edited my heart's voice with my mind. The mind can be our greatest ally or our biggest enemy, depending on how much we rely on its ideas. An idea is just an idea. A feeling is just a feeling. A behavior is just a behavior. And none of these are you. These concepts become more real to us beyond anxiety as detachment overtakes attachment in many, if not all, aspects of life.

To follow up on my original story about myself during and beyond anxiety, I progressively became more open to things going wrong and no longer clung to the need to have things go the right way. If it was an herb I was taking, I gave it time and no longer checked in every 5 minutes (hat was the truth during most anxiety-filled days) to see if it was working. The checking-in itself breeds more fear and pressure; hence the perpetual cycle of anxiety lives on. Rather, I naturally began focusing on the long-term potential of that herb and gave it months before I decided whether or not it worked. I engaged in shamanic practices around what is known as soul retrieval, but this time without expectation and pressures to heal this instant. I was compassionate toward the practice itself, the shaman, and myself. My reward was clarity and an overall feeling of emotional, physical, and spiritual progress. It was amazing. I got myself to the point where I would set a goal for myself, and whether I reached it or not, I was OK with it; I was fulfilled by the process.

You can imagine the pressure that was being lifted through this transition that I was in. It is a beautiful thing to be a part of, and since this book is here to give you a glimpse of what to expect during and after the anxiety-healing journey, I'm deeply excited for what is to come in your life. I more clearly could see what was toxic in my life and what wasn't. At the time, however, because I was living in survival mode, I worshipped my boss and co-workers because being laid off would mean the worst. This mindset kept my low self-worth alive and strengthening over time. During anxiety, it can be challenging to see beyond our survival-based thinking patterns, but beyond anxiety, we are much more sensitive to this information. We go from one type of sensitivity to another. One where we look to keep things as they are no matter what (during anxiety) to sensing and trusting that letting go will lead to where we're truly meant to go (beyond anxiety). Think about it; every result in your life was met with an initial feeling of being ecstatic for your achievement, followed by emotional neutrality, followed by setting the bar even higher. The real question here should be: Are we chasing a desire or just a feeling? I would say, a feeling.

Everything we do is so that we can feel more of one thing and less of another.

Everything else in between is just details—details we place a tremendous amount of importance on but have no importance within them whatsoever. As with all the changes coming your way during the anxiety-healing process, you must fully open your arms up to them. You *will* change. Are you OK with that? Actually, let me rephrase that. You and your entire world will change! Your posture, your vocabulary, your interests, your circle of friends, your family dynamic, your career, your diet, your living location, and your God will change. Will you stand in the way of that, or will you get out of the way? If you stand in the way of change, you will be met with a familiar future, one in which you have a small life experience. If you get out of the way, you will be met with an unfamiliar future, one in which every day will feel like a new life. Yesterday truly doesn't exist anymore at this point in your journey because your curiosity about what will happen today takes over like an uncorrupted child who can't wait to meet with new life experiences. As we move from being childish (set in our old ways) to being childlike (living life on our own terms), the process is fun, not draining. We may take a 40-minute bike ride through a long and narrow bridge, and we're no longer focusing on the satisfaction of getting to our destination but rather the satisfaction of being here and now, on the bridge, as an example.

Beyond anxiety, we realize that there is as much learning to be done while not doing anything as there is while we are engaged in doing something. The Italians call it "the art of doing nothing," and these words have been a staple of my own belief systems for years now. Being fully present, preferably in a naturistic environment, will teach you things no book can ever teach you. That is because humans will never be able to find the words to express the deepest teachings that this outside intelligence offers. It's just not possible. We feel, we know, but we cannot fully express how we know and are learning, and that is OK. Even as I write this book for you, I am only sharing with you about 15% of what I know to be true about reality and this universe. Do I know much more? Definitely! Can I express it in a way that you may understand and I may wholeheartedly feel is right? I cannot. Many of the discoveries you need to tap into will be made through your own experience, not by anyone or anything else. Life will teach you how meaningless it is to cling to a result for the sake of feeling worthy and present. When life teaches, we must listen. As you can see with healing anxiety, we are not simply discussing a shift in your emotional state; we are looking at a total transformation happening right before your eyes. It's a beautiful and inspiring thing to witness, so continue to take those bold steps, and soon, you will only look back to see how far you've come on this journey.

Summary:

In this brief chapter, I wanted to help you understand the difference between focusing on a result and focusing on the process. There is no need to focus on the result because once you have any sort of result in mind, you get emotional around it. Any information that accompanies emotion gets stored deeper in the mind than information that lacks emotion, so the system already knows what you want. A natural byproduct of all these small wins over anxiety is trust, and trust leads to enjoyment around the process. If you're currently still feeling stuck in the grips of anxiety, you may feel an overwhelming need to focus on results and, therefore, are bypassing the necessary steps you need to be fully engaged with in order for the result to manifest. If this is the case, gently see that this is the case and bring yourself back to a more processed-focused approach.

Chapter 12 – The Love of Uncertainty

The fear of dying and the fear of poverty are now seen as learned, not real. Fear is hard-wired; irrational fear is learned.

There was a time during my anxiety disorder when I unconsciously sorted for certainty, and if it wasn't there, neither was I. I remember turning down career opportunities, social get-togethers, even walks on my own out of fear about what might happen. My imagination was very vivid back then. It still is now that I am beyond anxiety, but the difference is that during anxiety, I was unconsciously imagining the worst possible outcome. Now, I consciously imagine the best. I remember my inner child creatively reminding me how I wasn't skilled enough at something, or it just wasn't the right time for a new career, so I backed out. Its response to my idea about taking a walk on my own was that I would be seen as a loner, a loser, so I backed away. Every time my adult, more experienced mind became curious about what a new experience or habit would be like, the inner child reminded me that uncertainty meant pain and suffering, and so I followed that voice.

It wasn't until I reminded myself of everything I would regret lying on my death bed years from now that I began shifting my association toward uncertainty.

Regret is a great motivator and one that many anxiety sufferers use today to open up to new behaviors and habits. When you stop to consider everything you're missing out on while you manage and babysit your anxiety symptoms day after day, anger and dissatisfaction begin to arise. These reminders must be present daily though otherwise, it will become too easy to fall back into the addiction to suffering and anxiety. Beyond anxiety, there is no difference between certainty and uncertainty, control and a lack of control, familiar and unfamiliar. It's all just connected to life. Why strive for certainty when uncertainty is where the lessons and memories live? This is an important question, as it begins the process of letting go to change.

Some things are just not meant to be understood.

Yet, we strive to understand. We fight harder and harder for an answer to our inner questions around anxiety, only to find more answers. Overthinking is the enemy in this journey, and it is perpetuated by an unconscious desire to keep things as they are. To fall in love with uncertainty, you must fall in love with vulnerability. To be vulnerable is scary at first and pleasant over time. Do not shy away from feeling vulnerable. Welcome it, get to know it, allow it to stay. In time, you will open yourself up while feeling vulnerable, which proves to the subconscious mind that it is safe to move toward positive change.

One example of this from my own life was speaking in front of a crowd. My inner child would always create some kind of injury or sickness prior to having to speak in front of crowds as a safety response to an outcome that I may regret in the future. Nowadays, beyond anxiety, I no longer experience this same psychological and physiological response because my inner child and adult mind are working as a team, not against each other anymore. When I think about speaking in front of crowds, whether that's online during a monthly masterclass or in person, I am reminded that it has much more to do with others than myself. There is no feeling of vulnerability because these types of situations are now seen from a much broader point of view. We fear vulnerability because we are afraid of making mistakes since we feel like we've already made so many during our childhood years. Letting others down is a common fear that many anxiety sufferers live with, and it is not justified. It is not justified because over-generalization is a common theme with anxiety. We think we always do the wrong thing or always fail while taking on a new endeavor when, in fact, these are moments you could count on one hand alone. It's the over-generalization that brings us back to our comfort zones, back to familiarity, and farther away from the inspiration that comes with uncertainty.

Uncertainty inspires while certainty restricts.

We mustn't forget, however, that everyone's healing journey is different. One person's introduction to uncertainty and a shift in emotional association toward it may need to be very gradual compared to another person who has reached the point of "no return." When one is beyond anxiety, it's important to still place ourselves in the psychology and physiology of an anxiety sufferer at times to truly understand what it is still like for others since it can be easy to forget. I know for myself that there are certain foods and stimulants that have the potential to bring me some degree of anxiousness when needed, and I continue from time to time to sit with and fully experience these anxious moments deliberately for the sake of deeper understanding when working with others through my programs. I would only recommend this deliberate dive back into anxiety symptoms for other coaches and healed individuals who have a very firm understanding of their new identities. If not, the potential to backtrack through one idea that compounds into others will still be there.

Uncertainty can be a friend rather than a foe.

This healing journey is all about rebuilding our relationships with our bodies, minds, people, environments, etc. When these relationships improve naturally, life provides us with more of its secrets. Secrets it would never have shared with us during anxiety because we would not be ready to receive them. It's the process of healing that brings about new wisdom and knowledge. It's like lottery winners who receive a lump sum of money without being ready for it. They spend it quickly, and many of them are more broke within a few years than they were before they won the lottery. Their minds and instincts overtake their intuition, which leads them down the path of temporary bliss only to be met with a tremendous low soon after. These aren't bad people; they just haven't created enough awareness in their lives to recognize the difference between an instinctual decision from an intuitive one.

An instinctual decision comes from the beliefs of the inner child, who believes that the world is an unsafe place. An intuitive decision comes from an intelligence source within you that looks to align itself with the way nature lives and thrives. The tree that is immovable; the path that doesn't restrict who walks on it; the leaves that fall from a branch not striving and fighting to get back on; the river that flows between rocks without any complaints as to why they're in the way. If you live by the rules of your instincts, you will trick yourself into thinking that you must compete with everything, hence the never-ending state of standing guard against anything the feels wrong. If you live by the rules of your intuition, you will make peace with what you once feared and hated, and your life will be centered around compassion and connectedness with all things. This will lead you toward a flow state. This flow state represents progress and a balance between willpower and allowance. When the right time is to do the right thing, you will know; and when the right time is to lay low and allow something to manifest when it is meant to, you will know.

"Only he who, himself enlightened, is not afraid of shadows." — Immanuel Kant

Within this context, those shadows that Kant is referring to are within uncertainty. We live in uncertain times; this is the truth. Uncertain times and uncertain moments demand enlightened beings. People need people to lead them, to help them see what they cannot in the moment. This is where you and I are called to rise up. As humans who've lived through an anxiety disorder and are ready to share the lessons that we've compiled along the way, we have a duty to the world. That duty is to be empathetic but not overly sympathetic since extreme sympathy can become a reason to keep an anxiety disorder alive for a sufferer, to receive what they truly wish to deep down. Beyond anxiety, we want to tell others that it's OK to dance, sing, paint, smile, laugh spontaneously, etc. Nothing beautiful needs a reason to show up anymore. Deep down, we are all artists who have become far too robotic. To let our artistry shine as it may gives light to the darkness, and soon we become much more expressive than we ever have been. Remember what I mentioned earlier in this book, that expression is freedom while suppression is anxiety and suffering. Promise yourself that you will embrace uncertainty with an open heart from this day forward, and your life's journey will be magical. You have this potential within you, so guide the doubt when it arises, express those beautiful words when the time is right, and become more than anxiety one small win at a time.

Summary:

Leaving the world of robotic consciousness takes steady intention. At the start of each day, do not wish for a day without challenges but instead intend to be equipped with the inner resources needed when challenges of the day arise. This practice will open you up to perceiving the "bad" as being neutral and the neutral to being "good." As you move beyond anxiety, you will be equipped with a nonjudgmental approach toward uncertain future experiences. This is a natural result of the targeted inner work you have been doing.

Chapter 13 – Final Words: Where to go Beyond Anxiety?

To build on the words from the start of this book … before anxiety, there is ignorance; during anxiety, there is learning, and after anxiety, there is momentum. Warrior, the positive momentum in your life is building, and it's up to you to continue to water this plant every day for the rest of your life. Where you go from here depends on the guidance from your intuition. No matter what, it is creative, and it will continue to challenge you. You may feel a push to write your own book about your journey, help others who have suffered like you, or simply allow your presence to unconsciously pass inspiring information to others without uttering a single word to them. No matter what the voice of your heart says, it's up to you to listen and execute. The only way to fall back into a world of anxiety is when an initial limiting idea or feeling grows. I trust that you feel you are beginning to guide that voice and feeling much better than you have before, and for that, I am so proud of you.

Become the master of your own destiny.

For this, you will come to the realization that the vast majority of the time, you will disagree with the way larger groups think and act. This is natural beyond anxiety—it's to be expected. It's your divine path to separate from the majority and connect with the minority now. Anxiety is perpetuated by intelligence, which many times has an immediate connection to instinct. The more we look to understand things through our intellect, the more we wish we could go backward and set the intention for our intuition to guide us toward the answer instead. You are a co-creator of your reality; the meaning of your co-partner in this healing journey is up to you. Some may call it God. No matter what you call it, it is correct for you. We, as former anxiety sufferers, have been brutally bent but never broken. We've found ways to bend ourselves back into someone we never thought we'd be, and because of this, you and I will have a lasting bond forever. Even if I don't know you personally, I am always with you, and you are with me, and that is a beautiful thing.

Love is about appreciation, so appreciate this journey you are on daily.

Without a sense of enjoyment and even fun, the positive momentum ends. Therefore, beyond anxiety, you must continue to allow these things to be present as you continue to mold yourself into the true light that you are. Seriousness blocks positive momentum; nothing needs to be taken seriously on this healing journey because once things get too serious, constriction arises once again. Remember, the mind and body are always in communication with one another. If the body constricts out of seriousness, so will the mind filter out optimism and possibility and begin filtering in pessimism, threats, fear, doubt, and so on. This is the price we pay for seriousness. Playfulness is something that you are or will begin adopting into your life. Playfulness leads to oxytocin saturation (the cuddle hormone). The more oxytocin, the more plastic our neurology gets (neuroplasticity), and the faster we create new belief systems. Orgasms, hugging, dark chocolate (minimal, of course), and laughter all help to create new neural pathways for new conditioning to take place. As you can see, these new traits and behaviors you are adopting not only have an immediate effect on your emotional state, belief system, and identity but a lasting effect as well.

From here on, you must give what you want to receive.

If it is self-love you want more of, you must provide this to others whether you know them or not and whether they're your friends or enemies. Beyond anxiety, we no longer have enemies, and we no longer put people into a bunch of separated compartments. Because we see the big picture in things, experiences that used to negatively affect us no longer do.

Take criticism, for instance. When someone criticizes me now, I wish them healing and inner peace. I understand that their words are not directed at me but are actually directed at mom, dad, uncle, doctor, teacher, or any other person in their lives that they haven't made peace with yet. To take critical words to heart shows that the person is still stuck in survival mode, survival thinking, and instinctual reactions. An initial reaction is fine, but it usually is followed up with a response soon after so that it helps to dissolve the animal instincts when they unnecessarily arrive. Remember, what you believe, you feel. So if you believe that people, in general, are against you and want the worst for you, then you will feel the weight of the world on your mind, body, and spirit. If you believe that people are for you and want to see you blossom like a beautiful flower, you will feel compassion and inspiration to take on any challenge that should arise. How you respond to a feeling in your body will determine your level of consciousness. So have the compassion to allow an instinctual feeling to be present initially and also have the awareness to see beyond the reaction. The moment of inner conflict holds the greatest opportunity for personal growth, which is why we must seize each opportunity and not wish for a straightforward life.

A warrior doesn't always win the battle, but it is definite that they will win the war.

There will be times when setbacks happen, and this is good. It does not mean that you need to change your "I am's," but rather, it means that life is looking to see how committed you truly are to change. The universe will certainly provide you with all you need and all you want. However, it will only provide you with the bare minimum until it senses that you feel you deserve and are creating enough momentum toward gaining it all. When you are actually living out the kind of life you want to live with a sense of certainty around your new identity, only then will the law of attraction (and other laws) work in your favor.

I kept this book short because that's what I sensed was the right thing to do. It's not the length of the information provided to a person looking for it but rather the right kind of information that's important. I wanted to give you a sense of what to expect during and after the healing process over anxiety has taken shape, and I hope I have been able to do that here in this book for you. Beyond anxiety, there are a few things I ask of you to keep the momentum going, and they are:

- Be a ready, fire, aim kind of person. Be an inherent action taker and never allow the editing process of your mind to lead you to doubt.
- Be open-minded. Go with the flow; be flexible and adaptable to life's circumstances.
- Be kind to yourself and create a nurturing inner environment. The inner dialogue between your experienced adult mind and your inner child must be gentle. Conscious thought and feeling must work in harmony.
- Release unimportant information. If it leads you down a path that reminds you of your anxiety days, let it go.
- Brush off failures. Because they never really are failures but more like hiccups.

We came to this world self-confident, and over time, we taught ourselves how to be afraid. Never again will we allow ourselves to be afraid of what doesn't truly justify these feelings and emotions. Rather, we are more than anxiety now, and with this presence comes the responsibility to live in line with these words. Promise to take on each day with curiosity and intent, and you will never go backward again.

Dennis Simsek

Made in the USA
Middletown, DE
28 June 2021